DECORATIVE
CACTI

DECORATIVE CACTI

A Guide to Succulent House Plants

Text by Rudolf Šubík
Illustrations by Jiřina Kaplická

Spring Books

Translated by
Olga Kuthanová

Designed and produced by
Artia for Spring Books
Published by
The Hamlyn Publishing Group Limited
London · New York · Sydney · Toronto
Hamlyn House, Feltham, Middlesex, England
© Copyright Artia 1971

Reprinted 1972

ISBN 0 600 31672 6

Printed in Czechoslovakia

Cacti and Succulents

Every plant needs not only light, heat, air and nutrients for its life processes, but also water. Large areas the world over suffer from a dire lack of moisture and the rainfall in such places is usually limited to one or several brief periods. Even so, there is no absence of vegetation, though it is restricted to plants that have become adapted to the difficult conditions and have learned to overcome them.

Plants exposed to excessive aridity and a scorching sun transform their bodies into reservoirs of water. They are further adapted to their habitat by the shape of the body and the composition and form of growth which limit evaporation to the minimum. Such plants commonly found on the European continent are *Sedum, Sempervivum, Caralluma* and the like. In warmer zones there are far more of these plants, called succulents because their parts are juicy and fleshy (the Latin word *succus* means juice).

Typical plants of this group are the cacti, even though they form only a small part of all the succulents. Cacti are best adapted with the shape of the body to the conditions in which they grow and therefore many other exotic succulents of like shape are mistakenly believed to be cacti even though they belong to another family; for example, the agave, which belongs to the same family as the narcissus, or aloes and haworthias, members of the lily family which also includes the lily-of-the-valley and the tulip. The greatest leaf succulence is shown in the South African genera *Lithops, Conophytum*, etc., where the whole plant consists of two, joined leaves only an inch or so high.

Organography of Cacti

Forerunners of the cacti probably grew in the damp tropical forests and resembled the majority of present-day plants. In time, however, they spread to areas changed by lengthening periods of drought into prairies and deserts and gradually adapted themselves to these inclement conditions. The shape of the body and all the body organs underwent marked changes, traces of which are manifest in today's cacti. *Peireskia* and certain of the *Opuntia*, for instance, possess in the early stage of growth organs resembling leaves, whereas most other cacti have only infinitesimal scales, for the function of leaves (namely assimilation and transpiration) was taken over by the thick, green stem.

The globose, ovate or columnar body of the cactus provides a maximum store of water and minimum evaporation surface. Loss of water is further limited by the thickened skin, often covered with a wax coating. The stomatal pores necessary for transpiration are few and deeply set. The body tissues contain mucus which binds water. Besides this the plant surface is covered with dense spikes, hairs or wool as protection against heat or cold. Everything serves to economize water so that the cactus might survive a drought of several months' or even several years' duration. This characteristic is a favourable one for the European cactus grower for he can go away for a summer holiday without having to worry that his specimens will become too dry and he can also see them through the winter without undue difficulty, since cacti are not watered during this period and may even be stored wrapped in paper and placed in a drawer in a dry, cold room.

Even more varied than the body shape is the size of cacti. These range from the smallest known species *Blossfeldia minima*, measuring about $\frac{1}{2}$ inch (1 centimetre), to the giant columnar cerei growing up to 65 feet (20 metres) in height and often branching out into large tree-like forms. The several-centuries-old barrel-shaped Mexican cacti, measuring more than 3 feet (1 metre) across and 6 feet (2 metres) in height, weigh more than 1 ton. The whip-like forest species hang in rich clusters from tall trees whereas other genera such as *Opuntia* have bodies consisting of flat, oval joints. Some cacti which once again found themselves back in a damp forest habitat, for example *Phyllocactus* and *Rhipsalis*, did not produce the leaves they had had in the earlier stages of evolution but their stems developed shapes very like leaves. This great diversity of shape and size, practically unequalled in the plant kingdom, is one of the reasons why cacti are so popular. The many miniature species make it possible to have an attractive and valuable collection of cacti even in the small space of a window-sill.

Besides the normal body shapes, the cactus family also has abnormal forms, the so-called monstrous forms and the more abundant pectinate or cristate forms.

In some instances, especially in the columnar cacti of the cereus group, the symmetrical, cylindrical growth around a vertical axis changes into an irregular, sectional growth giving rise to the so-called monstrous forms. These irregularly branched aberrations were much in demand for their strangeness and comparative rarity, especially because they can be grown from cuttings.

Far more common aberrations are the cristate forms where the growing point gradually turns into a growth line and the stem develops a so-called crest or fan. This change in growth, for which no fully satisfactory reasons have yet been found, may occur in young seedlings as well as in older plants where the tops of tall, columnar cacti spread out like fans. These cristate forms, which may occur in all species of cacti and other succulents, are highly prized by some collectors. In our collections these forms are propagated almost solely by grafting on tall stock on which the crests of the soft-fleshed species form twisted cornucopias and rich folds and those of the hard species straight, rigid combs. Cristates do not blossom, or if they do then only very little (with the exception of *Mammillaria zeilmanniana f. cristata* and certain other mammillarias), and are cultivated only for their peculiarity of shape.

The structure of a cactus is very ingenious. The soft, water-filled and therefore heavy bodies are supported by a woody portion. In most species the lower parts gradually turn woody throughout. In the tall columnar cacti the axial tissues soon turn woody, thus providing a firm support and assuring the plant's stability.

Great variety is also exhibited by the roots, which are adapted to the type of soil. Those growing in soil rich in humus form a fine dense network, whereas those growing in heavy soils are thick and little branched. Some cacti have turnip-like roots. These underground stores of water are often larger than the plant itself, the latter being pulled down into the earth in periods of excessive drought, as in the *Lophophora*. Cacti can send out roots not only from the cut surface of cuttings, but also from prostrate stems, individual joints, and sometimes even from every part of the body. This characteristic was instrumental in spreading certain opuntias which became domesticated in North Africa and southern Europe. In Australia it proved catastrophic, for opuntias here spread so rapidly and over such vast areas that they posed a serious threat to farming. The roots of cacti are usually fragile and break easily. For this reason it is necessary to take particular care when removing the plant from the soil and to abstain from watering the transplanted specimen for at least fourteen days so as to prevent the roots from rotting.

The surface of the stem is rarely smooth. As a rule it is made up of ribs which shade the body, permit it to shrink in periods of drought and also give it firmness. Ribs are themselves sometimes divided laterally by grooves to form tubercles or warts. The shapes of the ribs, tubercles and warts show the same diversity as the other plant organs. As tubercles are often to be found in the seedlings of cacti in which the adult form has clearly defined ribs, it can be deduced that in some species ribs evolved from the gradual joining of tubercles.

The chief vegetative centre in cacti, that is, the spot where the new cells are formed during the growing period, is the crown of the plant which is usually depressed as protection from the intense heat of the sun. Auxiliary vegetative points, however, are also to be found on other parts of the body surface, chiefly in the form of areoles which are regularly spaced on the edges of the ribs or on tubercles and are usually protected by wool and spines. In the majority of cacti areoles bear blossoms and shoots. In some cacti, as for example the *Mammillaria*, further vegetative points are the axils of the tubercles, and in others, like the *Coryphantha*, the grooves joining the areoles and axils, from all of which both flowers and shoots may arise.

The most constant decorative feature of cacti is their spines. These are widely varied in shape, size and colour and above all they are excellent protection. In shape they range from delicate, almost invisible down through long, thick hairs and bristles to spikes more than 6 inches (15 centimetres) long. The easily broken-off joints of some opuntias with delicate spines called glochids catch in the hair of animals or in the feathers of birds and are carried great distances. It is thus that opuntias spread all the way to Africa.

Young spines arising from the crown of the cactus often glow with colour; glassy transparency or snowy-white in some species, all shades of yellow and red, as well as brown or purplish-black to pure black. It was doubtless the bizarreness, colouring and size of the spines of the Mexican cacti, together with the magnificence of their blooms, that attracted the Spanish conquerors and later the first European collectors and growers. After the First World War it was chiefly the thick silvery hairs of the "Old Man", *Cephalocereus senilis*, that awoke a new interest in cacti, thus marking a new era of widespread cactus growing and collecting.

Only a few cacti are completely without spines. These are the epiphytic forest species, for example the genus *Rhipsalis*, or those that practise mimicry, hiding themselves amidst bare boulders and in the sand of the Mexican wastelands, like the *Ariocarpus, Lophophora,* etc. In these plants, as well as in the spineless species *Astrophytum myriostigma* and *A. asterias,* the spines are present in the early stages of seedling growth but later disappear.

For growers accustomed to handling them daily the spines of cacti are not too unpleasant and certainly not dangerous. The widespread belief that they are poisonous is just that — a belief. Unpleasant for the uninitiated, however, are the glochids of opuntias resembling miniature spines. The greatest attraction of the species *Opuntia microdasys* is the white, golden-yellow or brownish-red pillows on the areoles. These are made up of innumerable, almost microscopically fine, fragile glochids which cause unpleasant itching of the skin at the slightest contact. When handling these cacti, for example when transplanting, it is necessary to guard the eyes, for the glochids fill the air and could cause chronic inflammation.

Another even greater attraction of cacti, though more transitory, is the blossoms. These arise from the growing points, generally from the areoles but also from the axils (in mammillarias) and grooves (in coryphanthas), almost always one flower from one point. In some cacti the flowers appear on the crown (growing from the youngest areoles), in others on the sides (from older areoles). In some cases the plants have whole groups of flower-bearing points (mammillarias often produce wreaths of blossoms). Like the spines, the flowers also vary widely in shape and size as well as in the period of flowering and its duration. In size they range from the smallest blooms of mammillarias, only $\frac{1}{2}$ inch (1 centimetre) across, to the huge blossoms of the climbing cerei measuring about 16 inches (40 centimetres) across and the largest to be found in nature.

Just as varied is the range of colours comprising, besides pure blue hues, all possible shades including bright green in the species *Brasilicactus graessneri.* The delicate tones, silky sheen and brightness of the colours, not to be found in other plants, is what makes the blossoms of cacti so attractive. Also the violet tints in the throat of the *Phyllocactus hybridus* flower are a fascinating sight for anyone who has ever seen it.

Most cacti flowers open during the day and last from one day to one week, depending on the species and the weather. It is these diurnal blooms whose bright colours frequently attract insects or humming birds, thereby causing their pollen grains to be carried from one flower to another resulting in fertilization and the production of seed. Many cacti are self-pollinating. In some, like the genus *Frailea,* the seed is already present in the bud which changes into an ovary (so-called cleistogamy). The flowers, then, need not become fully developed. Then there are the many cacti whose flowers, generally white and fragrant but sometimes also putrid-smelling, open in the evening and die with the coming of dawn. These are the ones that are usually the largest and often the most beautiful, be they the common window-sill cacti of the genus *Echinopsis* or the well-known "Queen of the Night" whose large, glowing white bloom with its powerful scent attracts nocturnal pollinators. Flowers also vary in structure, ranging from those where the reproductive organs (stamens with anthers and style with stigma) protrude from a narrow perianth, to the nocturnal blooming cacti with large, wide-open flowers.

Like variation is to be found in the fruit of cacti which in some species is just as distinctive but a more lasting ornament than the flowers. The fruit of most cacti (with flowers growing from the areoles) is located on the areoles. In other species, for example the *Mammillaria*, they arise from the wool of the axils and in still others they are permanently concealed in the wool of the crown from which only the seeds protrude (as in the *Lophophora*). Most cacti have fleshy fruit, coloured green, yellow, red and white or violet, sometimes covered with a bluish bloom. Some burst or disintegrate when ripe, others are dry and crack or release the seed after shrivelling of the cover. The size of fruits also varies, ranging from small, inconspicuous dry fruit concealed in wool to ones as big as plums or even large apples (as in some of the cerei).

Seeds vary in size and structure and are so specific for each given species that they are one of the best and most reliable means of classification of the different genera and species. Seeds have a firm cover and are usually located in the sweet flesh of the ovary, welcome food of birds, which thus aids in the propagation of the plants. As a rule seeds germinate very quickly, within several days. The seedlings of cacti on the lower rungs of the evolutionary ladder have large seed leaves (the cacti are dicotyledons) whereas in those higher up they are suppressed and the germinating seeds do not have an elongate shape but resemble miniature marbles.

The Home of Cacti and Their Distribution

The original home of cacti is North and South America. Species growing in the wild elsewhere were probably brought there by birds (species of *Rhipsalis* occur both in Africa and India) or in more recent times by man. That is how the opuntias of southern Europe, Africa and Australia came into being.

In their native territory cacti are distributed over vast areas, especially in warm and dry regions. Some species, however, are to be found even in cold regions with severe frosts in winter and a climate far harsher than in Europe. In North America some opuntias have penetrated north of the 50th parallel all the way to the 60th parallel, which corresponds to the latitude of Stockholm. In South America some cacti occur even in the harsh and cold regions of Patagonia, from about 53° latitude north to 50° latitude south. The North American region with the greatest wealth of cacti is Mexico. It is the classic home of the cactus and has even incorporated this plant in its coat-of-arms.

Mexican species were the first to be collected, described and, alas, also removed in great numbers to Europe so that the government had to intervene by limiting or forbidding their export to prevent certain species from becoming extinct. Mexico is the home of the most remarkable cacti: *Astrophytum*, *Leuchtenbergia*, *Lophophora*, *Aztekium*, *Obregonia*, *Strombocactus*, as well as home of the majority of species of the genera *Mammillaria*, *Echinocereus*, *Echinocactus*, *Ferocactus*, *Thelocactus* and numerous others. It is here that the largest columnar and candelabra or tree-like cerei are to be found, and here, also, the most widespread stands of these cacti and opuntias, sometimes forming whole forests. Barrel-shaped species also attain gigantic dimensions in Mexico.

The south-western United States (California, Arizona, Texas) bordering on Mexico are the home of further genera and species of cacti, most of them of Mexican origin. As in Mexico these cacti, together with other prairie and desert plants (chiefly *Agave* and *Yucca*), have given these districts the characteristic appearance so well known from photographs, films and books. Cacti mainly occur here in inland regions, on the upland plateaus and in the mountains where there is slight rainfall, whereas in the hot, humid regions, especially near the coast, one will find only a few species.

North and east of these regions rich in cacti their numbers rapidly decrease. In Mississippi and Missouri only opuntias are to be found. In Central America, on the coast of the Gulf of Mexico and on its islands there are few cacti. Only some forest species such as the genera *Phyllocactus* and *Rhipsalis* grow here and various mellocacti and cerei.

A like situation is to be found in the tropical lands on the northern coast of South America. Besides the above species these regions also have occasional *Mammillaria*, *Frailea* and *Malacocarpus*. The types growing in the equatorial region bordering the river Amazon are limited to epiphytic cacti *(Phyllocactus, Rhipsalis)* and runner cerei. Brazil is also the home of the genera *Melocactus* and *Discocactus*. The drier plateaus in the south-east and especially the south abound in cerei and we begin to find members of the genera *Brasilicactus*, *Eriocactus*, *Notocactus* and *Gymnocalycium*.

In Ecuador, and especially in Peru and Bolivia, the number of cacti begins to increase from north to south, mainly high-mountain species such as *Lobivia*. On the high mountain plateaus of the Andes cacti reach as far as the snow line, that is, to elevations of 1,700 feet (5,000 metres). Alpine species of the genera *Tephrocactus* and *Oreocereus* are covered with a thick coat of wool and other genera such as *Lobivia*, *Rebutia*, *Aylostera*, *Oroya* and *Parodia* also have typical high-mountain members.

A large number of cacti is native also to Chile. The hard and as a rule dark, grey-green Chilean cacti are apparently the last dying remains of a once rich cactus population of this harsh land. This is the land of origin of the genera *Neoporteria*, *Eriosyce*, *Pyrrhocactus*, *Horridocactus* and other spherical cacti attractive to fanciers chiefly for their magnificent and unusually thick spines. Also to be found here are numerous cerei, opuntias, etc.

The majority of South American species, however, grow in Paraguay, Uruguay and above all Argentina. The greatest concentrations are to be found in the north-western province of Salta, which may be considered the South American pendant of Mexico. Miniature members of the genera *Rebutia* and *Aylostera*, the turnip-like lobivias, the numerous species of *Gymnocalycium* and *Parodia* simply abound in bright magnificent flowers and varieties of shapes. Among these one will also find large communities of giant columnar cerei of the species *Trichocereus pasacana*, the South American pendant of the famous tall candelabra species *Cephalocereus senilis* growing in Mexico's "Valley of Old Men". Also growing in Argentina are the majority of species of the genus *Echinopsis*, which includes the common window-sill species *Echinopsis eyriesii* with its large, fragrant white flowers, blooming, alas, only at night. Gymnocalycia grow throughout the whole of the country, all the way to harsh and cold Patagonia, where one will also find opuntias and austrocacti.

Characteristic cacti of Uruguay are the yellow-flowered and hard gymnocalycia, most notocacti, some species of the genus *Frailea*, the smallest cacti of all, malacocarpi and others. All of these spread to neighbouring Paraguay. Typical cacti of this country are certain miniature gymnocalycia (*Gymnocalycium damsii*, *G. anisitsii*, *G. mihanovichii*, etc.).

It is evident that in South America cacti are widespread over larger areas than in North America. These territories are located on either side of the equator and their climates are so diverse that it is impossible to state generally valid rules for the cultivation of the individual species growing here. Even though many hardy and rewarding plants have been brought to Europe from North America and Mexico (such as certain green *Mammillaria, Hamatocactus setispinus, Lophophora williamsii*), the number brought here from South America is even greater: members of the genera *Echinopsis, Gymnocalycium* or *Notocactus*, so well suited for all cactus growers including beginners, or the high-mountain genera *Lobivia, Rebutia, Aylostera* and *Parodia* which do best in the clean fresh air of the countryside. The reason for this is that the climate in some parts of Argentina is more like that of Europe than the climate of Mexico.

Although fashions in cactus growing vary as regards the popularity of the various succulents, there is no doubt but that the great variety that marks these plants is best shown in a collection which includes cacti from both Americas, showing also that both groups are equal. It is up to the grower to find out what groups, genera or even species of cacti or other succulents grow best in the conditions of his environment.

Growing Succulents

The first and foremost condition of successful growing is a true interest, which generally soon changes into a deep affection for these interesting plants. A further condition for success in cultivation is proper location and care, plus the selection of suitable types for the given environment.

A good cactus grower-collector knows without telling what his specimens need, and finds the types that will thrive in his environment. This can only be assured in a sunny site where there is direct sunlight for at least several hours a day. The more sunlight, the greater the selection of genera and species. A southern, unshaded situation is best, be it a window, balcony, glass case, greenhouse or hotbed. Fresh air is another must for successful cultivation. Protection from dust and the polluted air of large cities and industrial areas, adequate moisture and the required temperature can be provided only in a glass case, hotbed or greenhouse. Plants growing on window-sills suffer from one-sided light, even though they do quite well here.

In winter, the period of rest, a light, cool situation with a temperature of 10°C (50°F) is best. Smaller specimens are transplanted yearly, larger ones every three to four years into fresh, granular, porous soil. During the growing period they should be fertilized several times with a liquid fertilizer according to the enclosed instructions, the size of the plant, its condition, and the requirements of the individual species.

Watering is also of prime importance, determining the success or total failure of the specimen. It is governed by the season of the year, condition and size of the plant, and above all by the requirements of the individual species. In spring, when the cacti are awakened from their winter sleep, it is best to sprinkle them lightly until they show signs of growth. When incipient buds appear, the shrivelled stem fills out and the crown sprouts new spines. Water is applied liberally only when the bottom layers of soil have dried. If some cacti stop their growth water should be withheld for they are passing through the so-called summer dormant period. Late summer marks the onset of the autumn growth, water being applied again liberally until the end of September. After this the amount of water is gradually decreased until it is withheld altogether in the winter months. During this period only grafted plants are watered to keep the stock from becoming too dry. Other succulents are tended in the same manner.

The History of Cacti

Long before the advent of Europeans and the discovery of America, cacti were the subject of great interest on the part of the original inhabitants of that continent. This is quite understandable for they were plants that were an inseparable part of the landscape. The huge centuries-old columns and barrels of some species had withstood ages of the sun's heat and aridity of the desert as had no other known plants. Besides the ancient cult of peyote worship the ancient people of Mexico, especially the Aztecs, worshipped other species of cacti as well.

That is why we find many images of the cactus in the relics of the original Indians, especially in religious scenes. It seems that the large spherical Mexican cacti with thick spikes were used as sacrificial altars. Priests' assistants threw the naked bodies of the human sacrifices on to these huge, cruelly spiked plants before the high priest opened their chests with the knife to remove their hearts. Other scenes and ornaments also sometimes bore stylized likenesses of the spherical, columnar or jointed cacti.

Such remarkable and unusual plants, the likes of which were totally unknown in Europe, must have made an indelible impression on the Spanish conquistadors who first set foot on American soil. And cacti were naturally included among the rare oddities that they took home with them to Europe. The first references to these plants in literature date from the mid-16th century and have to do with the tree-like cerei, with their edible fruits called pitahaya by the natives, opuntias, whose crushed joints were used by the natives to heal bone fractures, and the melocacti of the West Indies, so striking with their brightly coloured caps (cephalia). *Phyllocactus phyllanthoides*, whose pink-flowering hybrids are to be seen on the window-sill of many a country or suburban home in Europe to this day, has also been cultivated on this continent for more than three hundred years.

At that time cacti were viewed only as strange plants that were the subject of distorted ideas and superstitions as regards their usage and true or possible healing effects. Only a few species were known in Europe, and not even thoroughly at that. This is borne out by the fact that Carl Linnaeus, the famous Swedish botanist who established the binomial nomenclature, knew only twenty-four species of cacti which he classed in one genus — *Cactus* (*cactos* is the Greek word for thistle). This was in the mid-18th century, and even in the years up to the French Revolution and the Napoleonic Wars there was no marked spread of the knowledge of cacti. Interest in these plants was restricted only to a few botanists and a few collectors, mainly in aristocratic circles, for it was a very expensive hobby. The period following the Napoleonic Wars up to the 1850s, the so-called Biedermayer era terminated by the revolutionary year of 1848, marked an upsurge in the popularity of cactus growing when this interest began to spread to the ranks of the townspeople, though the prime collectors continued to be the members of the nobility.

Cacti growing reached the height of its popularity in the last decades of the 19th century, which was also the period of a new interest in the arts and sciences in most countries of Europe. Cacti were cultivated not only by townspeople but the better known species also became stand-bys along with begonias, myrtle and passion flowers on the window-sills of suburban homes and even in villages, where to this day one will find very old specimens of *Echinopsis eyriesii* and *Phyllocactus ackermannii*. The comparatively short twenty-year period between the two world wars marked a rebirth of the popularity of cactus growing, which was becoming a hobby of the general public, people who could not afford to buy the costly plants imported from Mexico. This period is marked not only by a new system of cactus classification, but also by the great enlargement of collections resulting from the discovery of further new finds in the mountains of South America. The past decades have witnessed a marked increase in the number of growers, as a result of a better knowledge of cactus cultivation, improvements in their propagation from seed, both imported and home-grown, as well as in grafting, chiefly of seedlings. This made possible the acclimatization of even the rarest species which in the days of imported specimens were considered impossible to grow, like the melocacti.

Shortly before World War II the cactus-growing vogue of 1920—1935 began to show a downward trend, but it remained the foundation for the further upsurge of this hobby in the following years. It not only made possible the systematic exploration of whole districts of South America, but also the establishment of a large number of excellent collections, many of which survived the severe winters and air raids of the latter war years.

This brings us to the latest period of cactus growing and research, which is a fairly smooth continuation of the past periods, even though the war years marked a certain stagnation that was successfully overcome.

The Importance and Uses of Cacti

Growers find succulents attractive for their exotic origin and the vast range of shapes, making it possible to have in a very small area a large collection of hardy and rewarding plants bringing joy to the heart for many, many years.

Whereas in Europe they serve merely a decorative function, in their native habitat they are of far greater significance. Often they are the only vegetation on the vast expanses of arid land and some have many uses, though others, chiefly opuntias, are considered a troublesome weed.

The fruits of some cerei and opuntias, as large as a hen's egg, are not only a delicacy in Mexico and Brazil but often a welcome contribution to the diet, what with their abundance of refreshing juice. The fruits of cacti ripen during the dry season when the crops have already been harvested. During severe droughts not only the fruit but also the fleshy stem has been known to save both man and beast from dying of thirst.

Some kinds of opuntias were cultivated as fruit trees in America even before the coming of the Europeans and it was for this purpose that the Spaniards also took them home with them. They then became acclimatized in all of southern Europe and North Africa and even ran wild. The fruit of cacti is sold on the markets of small Mexican villages to this day. Besides being eaten fresh they are also preserved with sugar or made into alcoholic drinks, like the well-known "pulque" made from the juice of the agave.

16

The juice of some cacti contains substances which can have a beneficent or harmful effect on the human organism. Thus, for instance, some mammillarias and cerei contain alkaloids which cause cramps. Best known are the effects of the alkaloids of *Lophophora williamsii* and *L. lewinii*. Known as lophophorin, anhalonin and mescalin, these alkaloids produce sound and colour hallucinations. That is why the said cacti, called "peyotl" by the natives, were used long past either in the dried form, so-called "mescal buttons", or as a brew in religious festivities. The cult of lophophora or peyote worship is the subject of extensive literature and dried "mescal buttons" are the subject of a lucrative business to this day. On the other hand, the glucoside contained in the juice of *Selenicereus grandiflorus* is used in the treatment of heart disease.

In their native land, however, cacti can be of use to man in many other ways. Hedges of closely set cerei form impenetrable pallisades (*Marginatocereus marginatus* is used for this purpose in Mexico). Opuntias likewise provide inexpensive means of marking the boundaries of property or separating the pavement from the road in cities.

In barren, treeless areas, which are the rule in cactus-growing regions, the woody parts of the plant can serve not only as a substitute for fuel but also to build houses. This wood is light but tough, the structure of the tissues giving it the required firmness. That is why natives living in the regions where the giant columnar *Trichocereus pasacana* grows have used this cactus to build their huts for ages past.

In the days when aniline dyes were still unknown *Opuntia coccinelifera* was used as a host plant for the large-scale breeding of the insect which yields the valuable red colouring matter cochineal.

In regions where there is a lack of fodder for cattle, spineless opuntias are cultivated for this purpose, for example in northern Brazil. Even though it is an emergency measure, the importance of cacti as fodder cannot be underestimated.

Other succulents of economic importance are certain species of *Agave*, whose dried fibres are used in the production of ropes, sacks, nets, etc. The juices of these plants are used to make the alcoholic drinks pulque, mescal and tequila. The flesh of cacti preserved in sugar, like candied fruit, can be purchased even in the markets of large North American cities. Of late, the juice of the African *Aloe arborescens* is being used in the lay treatment of cancer.

It is thus evident that cacti and other succulents are not just useless prickly plants but that they served many significant purposes in the past and after more detailed research will doubtless be of importance in the future as well.

PLATES

Astrophytum asterias (ZUCC.) LEM.

The genus *Astrophytum* has always held a special place amongst cacti, even though it has no more than ten basic species, spread throughout eastern and northern Mexico.

Astrophytum asterias is one of the most remarkable species of the whole genus and besides that it also has an interesting history in that it was discovered twice. The first time by chance in 1843 by Baron Karwinski in the mountainous coastal region of north-east Mexico. The specimens brought to Europe, however, soon died and as Karwinski failed to define the exact location of the discovery site the species became a legendary plant preserved only in the form of a prepared specimen in the Munich botanical garden.

It was discovered a second time in 1943 when A. Frič recognized it amidst a fresh collection of cacti in the botanical garden in Mexico City. He made inquiries as to where the lot had been collected and was thus able to rediscoyer *A. asterias* and its original habitat. In the wild this plant can be found only after rain when it drinks up the water and flowers, for in dry periods it is pulled down into the ground.

These cacti were imported to Europe by the thousand, but apparently not a single one has survived to this day. *A. asterias* bore profuse blooms and cactus growers soon learned to propagate it from the seed, thus succeeding in saving this lovely species for us to cultivate.

The true *A. asterias* is a flat, compressed plant, up to 9½ inches (24 centimetres) across in its native habitat, with eight ribs. Down the centre of each rib is a line of spineless areoles and the hard skin of the entire plant is dotted with white wool. The large yellow flowers usually have a reddish throat. *A. asterias*, which was also found anew in southern Texas, is nowadays imported from American horticultural establishments in small numbers and will always remain a showpiece in our collections.

Astrophytum capricorne (DIETR.) BR. et R.

Whereas *A. myriostigma* and *A. asterias* are completely spineless, the species discovered at a later date do have spines. One of these is *Astrophytum capricorne*, so called for its blunt, curving spines, often twisted like the horns of an animal; the specific name *capricorne* means "goat-horned". This small, eight-ribbed cactus was discovered in 1851 by the physician Dr. H. Poselger, who had a large collection in Berlin and himself came to Mexico to collect cacti. Of all astrophyta this has the loveliest and largest flowers, up to 3 inches (8 centimetres) across, coloured a glowing yellow with carmine throat. The silky gloss is particularly marked in full sunlight. The adult plant has a somewhat columnar growth and attains a height of 10 inches (25 centimetres). The spines, up to ten to an areole, are flat and flexible, up to 3 inches (8 centimetres) long and $\frac{1}{10}$ inch (2 millimetres) wide. In age their originally brown colour turns to grey, the spines become fragile and break off easily so that older plants usually have spines only on the crown. Seedlings produce spines at a fairly late stage. The fruit of this species is also very different from that of the other astrophyta. It is longer and coloured red inside. *A. capricorne* matures comparatively early, this being the case particularly in the smaller variety *A. capricorne* var. *minor*, attaining only half the size of *A. capricorne* var. *major*. The smaller variety has a greater number of spines which appear already in the young seedlings and do not break off in age. It flowers, sometimes, as early as in the second year, especially if it is grafted. It is recommended to graft *A. capricorne* in any case, for older plants frequently lose their roots and as a rule the grower does not succeed in getting them to take root again. *A. capricorne* and the species *A. niveum* are the most delicate of the astrophyta. The hardiest and best growers of this genus are *A. ornatum*, *A. myriostigma* and *A. senile*. Another of the rarest species, next to *A. niveum*, is *A. crassispinum*, resembling *A. capricorne* but bearing flowers without the red throat. *A. asterias* ranges about midway on the list of the above species as regards its requirements and its difficulty to cultivate.

Astrophytum myriostigma LEM.

What with their hard skin, often covered with grey-white felted spots, and especially the odd shapes of their stems, astrophyta look more like petrified sea animals (particularly starfish and sea-urchins) than living plants. It is this that has marked them apart from the other members of the family Cactaceae and made them the elite amongst cacti, be it the "Bishop's Cap" *A. myriostigma*, the flat *A. asterias*, chalk-white *A. coahuilense*, golden-spined columnar *A. ornatum*, or *A. capricorne* with its grey, black or gold-tinged spines.

A collection of astrophyta will always be an object of interest on the part of cactus growers and admiration on the part of laymen for whom these hard plants are the epitome of the "true" cactus, unlike the soft-fleshed South American miniatures which cannot attract such interest except when in flower.

A. myriostigma is one of the oldest-known astrophyta with numerous varieties or geographical forms. It is not difficult to imagine the joy of the young botanist Galeotti when this lovely star-shaped cactus was discovered in 1837. As a rule, *A. myriostigma* has five ribs and is thickly spotted with felt, though four-ribbed, nude (only green) plants are not unknown. In their native habitat some varieties have a columnar growth almost 3 feet (1 metre) high and in age the number of ribs increases to eight. The flowers are pale glossy yellow. This species can be grown fairly well in Europe from the seed and need not be grafted. There is no more attractive sight than a bowl of well-cultivated *myriostigma* "caps". Those who fear the delicacy of the roots of older plants are advised to graft younger specimens on *Echinopsis*, providing them with ample sun under glass in summer and absolute lack of water in winter. This will assure their attaining a ripe old age.

Aylostera kupperiana (BÖD.) BACKBG.

The genus *Aylostera* embraces small, round to elongate cacti growing as single specimens or in groups, and with tubercles instead of ribs. Previously known species were classed in the genus *Rebutia*.

The species *Aylostera kupperiana* was discovered by F. Ritter in 1931 in Bolivia near Tarija where it grows on the walls of cliffs at a height of 8,000 feet (2,500 metres). It was so named in honour of Prof. Kupper.

The small globose stem is later columnar, coloured green, bronze with a purplish tinge in the sun. The low, spiralled tubercles have short white radial spines. The four central spines are $\frac{3}{4}$ inch (2 centimetres) long and coloured dark brown. The flowers are abundant, about $1\frac{1}{2}$ inches (4 centimetres) across and vermilion to bright orange-red. *A. kupperiana* is propagated in the same way as *Rebutia*.

Rebutia marsoneri WERD.

Rebutia marsoneri is a good plant for cultivation where there is little room and not much heat. The globose stem, $2\frac{1}{2}$ inches (6 centimetres) high and 3 inches (8 centimetres) across, is thickly covered with thin, glowing yellow spines up to $\frac{3}{4}$ inch (2 centimetres) long. The flowers are golden yellow, up to $1\frac{1}{2}$ inches (4 centimetres) across. They open in early spring. The plant was so named in honour of O. Marsoner who discovered it together with H. Blossfeld in Argentina in 1935.

The discovery of the golden-flowered *Rebutia* created a sensation among cactus growers for hitherto known species had borne only red blossoms. Further yellow-flowered specimens were discovered after a time by E. Vatter. Many are still without name, being assigned only a number, but they are so much alike that their differentiation is almost impossible.

Rebutias grow well in well-aired soil, in low boxes or bowls, always in groups of several specimens. After a brief period of rest in summer, growth is resumed at the end of August, the time for transplantation. In winter it should be kept in a cool room, temperature of 5°C (41°F), and dry atmosphere.

Cephalocereus senilis (HAW.) PFEIFF.

In its native habitat in Mexico this cactus forms huge, columnar stems rising to a height of 50 feet (15 metres) and measuring 12 inches (30 centimetres) in diameter. These branch at the bottom and have many low ribs. The whole is covered with wavy, white or grey hairs, $2\frac{1}{2}$—5 inches (6—12 centimetres) in length. The flowers emerge from a huge cephalium, that is, a thick fleece of spines on the crown. The flowers, appearing only after the stem has attained a height of 20—27 feet (6—8 metres), are bell-shaped, about $2\frac{1}{2}$ inches (6 centimetres) across, coloured pale pink. The fruit is large, round or oval with violet flesh.

Cephalocereus senilis (the specific name *senilis* means old) is a very popular cactus which launched the cactus-growing vogue following the First World War. Thousands of specimens were brought to Europe from Mexico, mostly shoots intended for the decoration of homes. These plants, accustomed to the hot Mexican sun, soon died in the dark houses and flats in towns. It was feared that their continual replacement with new specimens would in time cause their complete disappearance from their native habitat and that was why the Mexican government was forced to prohibit the export of cacti, including the species *Cephalocereus senilis*. The high cost of shipping the comparatively large plants was another reason why attempts were soon made to propagate the "Old Man" from seed, whereby cactus growers were gradually able to meet the demand for this lovely species.

Cephalocereus senilis was first exhibited as a great rarity at the Paris World Exhibition in 1889.

Propagation is not difficult. The "Old Man" thrives in porous, clay soil and is grafted only occasionally. During the growing period it requires adequate heat, sun and water. In winter it needs light, a dry atmosphere and temperature of 10—15°C (50—60°F).

28

Chamaecereus silvestrii (SPEG.) BR. et R.

Ch. silvestrii is usually to be seen on the window-sills of country houses together with *Echinopsis* and nutmeg. The stem is caespitose, comprising several soft, fleshy, pale green joints, ½ inch (1—1.5 centimetres) thick and up to 4 inches (10 centimetres) long. The ribs are practically unnoticeable with low tubercles covered with felt and ten to fifteen thin, grey-white spines. The flowers are funnel-shaped, 1½—2 inches (3—5 centimetres) long and the same across, vermilion on the inside. The native habitat is Argentina, Province of Tucuman and Salta.

Even though *Ch. silvestrii* is a common cactus it is highly appreciated for its hardiness and proliferous flowering, the dozens of vermilion bells appearing in early spring on slender shoots being a sight to truly gladden the heart. Many a cactus grower will remember that his first specimen was *Ch. silvestrii* given to him by a neighbour in the form of a shoot.

It is grown with ease in soil rich in food material, as a rule on window-sills where there is adequate light, heat and water. In winter the plant should be kept in the cold (the temperature may drop as low as 0°C (32°F) without causing any grave damage). A cool and dry environment is propitious for flower bearing, whereas in dry and warm surroundings the plant is susceptible to attacks of the red spider which causes ugly rust-brown spots on the plant. C. Backeberg introduced the form *Ch. crassicaulis cristata*. Available at the dealers is the popular yellow *Ch. silvestrii aurea*, which requires grafting. Propagation is easy — from the joints, which break off easily, or by grafting on thick stock of certain cerei. The specific name of the cactus is after the zoologist **Dr. Silvester**.

Echinocereus pulchellus (MART.) K. SCH.

Echinocereus pulchellus is a fairly popular and next to *E. pectinatus* the most widespread representative of the genus.

In former days this species was imported to Europe by the thousand but the prohibition of the export of cacti from Mexico and the discovery of new genera and species in South America caused the classic land of cacti to be ignored for a time. Nevertheless, the old and tried Mexican species have held their ground despite the vagaries of fashion in cactus growing.

One of these is *E. pulchellus* (the specific name *pulchellus* means beautiful) from San Luis Potosí, Mexico. The stem is spherical or short cylindrical at first, later producing shoots and forming groups up to 4 inches (10 centimetres) high. The crown is blue-green, the bottom of the stem pale green with a purplish tinge. The ribs are straight or spiral, divided into small tubercles. The spines, usually three to five, are whitish, about ½ inch (1 centimetre) long. The flowers are large, tinted with violet or pinkish violet with a dark central stripe, about 1½ inches (4 centimetres) across, with a distinctive, green ovary. They open in sunlight and last several days.

Commonly cultivated in collections is the variety *E. amoena*, which differs only slightly from the type plant and is therefore often mistaken for *E. pulchellus*. All echinocerei have attractive, large, generally violet-pink flowers, in some species up to 3 inches (8 centimetres) across, distinguished by a green ovary. These will survive long periods of drought and high temperatures as well as full sun in the summer season. In winter they withstand even below zero temperatures without damage. During the growing period they should be placed in full sun and given plenty of air and water. In winter they require a dry, light and cool environment. Propagation is generally by seed.

Echinofossulocactus pentacanthus   (LEM.) BR. et R.

The comparatively long and difficult to pronounce generic name of these unusual cacti, a rarity in the pure form today, at one time read *Stenocactus,* a much simpler and more apt designation in that it expressed the most typical characteristic of the plant, namely its markedly thin ribs. In almost all species these are very numerous and densely set like accordion pleats, sometimes wavy. In some cases their number exceeds one hundred, even though the plants in question are fairly small. Most species exhibit mutual transitions and numerous hybrids abound in the wild. The comparatively small flowers rise from the crown, and are coloured a nondescript whitish, yellowish, reddish to violet hue. Despite this, the genus *Echinofossulocactus* comprises some very interesting plants that can be grown without difficulty in a small space in slightly acidic soil. The plants' most decorative feature is the spines which are also the best means of identifying the various species. These cacti should be collected by every grower who wishes to enjoy the great variety of cacti and whose collection should embrace several of these typical plants which number about thirty-five species in all.

Echinofossulocactus pentacanthus was described more than a hundred years ago. The stem is small and pear-shaped with twenty-five to fifty ribs and a small number of areoles bearing five grey-black, flat spines. The broadest and longest point upwards. The flowers are fairly large, the whitish petals tinged with violet and with a central purple stripe. The native habitat is Hidalgo, Mexico, where it is even supposed to form groups made up of flat heads. Today it is impossible to state whether this is a species that is identical with *E. obvallatus* or one closely allied to other species. This, however, is an uncertainty encountered in many *Echinofossulocactus.*

Echinopsis eyriesii (TURP.) ZUCC.

Echinopses are South American cacti lacking the decorative stems of their Mexican counterparts but making up for this by being a richer green, as they grow in much richer soil, damper climate and are better protected against a scorching sun than their North American brethren. Echinopses as well as most other South American cacti thus have every reason to become ideal plants for beginners in Europe for they do not require glasshouse cultivation and do well under almost any conditions. Cultivation, of course, has been greatly facilitated by the efforts of generations of growers in cross-breeding and by numerous small growers who preserved ancient specimens through propagation from the shoots of the original plants and cultivation in nourishing fertilized soil. That is how these exotic cacti came to be common household plants in Europe, their lovely nocturnal blooms turning many a spectator into a would-be cactus collector and making them a favourite even with the more experienced.

Echinopsis eyriesii has a globose stem about 8 inches (20 centimetres) across in the juvenile form, becoming columnar in age, often attaining a height of more than 3 feet (1 metre). The ribs are prominent, dark green, with large, white-felted areoles bearing short spines. The flowers are white, tubular, up to 10 inches (25 centimetres) long, and bloom at night.

The native habitat of this frequently cultivated cactus is Brazil, Uruguay and Argentina. Propagation is easy — from shoots or from the seed.

Epiphyllum hybridum (Phyllocactus hybr.)

The history of the genera *Epiphyllum* and *Zygocactus* is already a known fact. For many decades cacti of the first genus and their hybrids were grown in Europe under the name *Phyllocactus* and the second genus was known under the name of *Epiphyllum* whereas in America the members of both genera were better known under the names favoured by today's botanists.

Wild epiphytes are cacti which, in the damp rain forests where these epiphytic plants are often found growing in the tops of palm and other trees, acquired a flattened shape showing a marked resemblance to leaves. These cacti are grown mainly for their magnificent flowers. Hybridization has produced blooms of such a size as can easily vie with the largest to be found amongst not only cacti but all other plants. Other specimens bear smaller flowers but in such profusion that not even orchids can stand up to them. The epicacti vogue in Europe has already passed, but in America these plants are still highly prized and are called "Orchid Cacti".

In Europe hybrids were cultivated by the English, French and Germans, who succeeded in growing hundreds of magnificent plants, some of which were so highly valued and considered such great rarities that they never appeared on the market. These included specimens with flowers measuring more than 12 inches (30 centimetres) across and with marvellous colour combinations; the "Blue Cross", for example, has the fine lines of a blue cross in the throat of its red blossoms, and there are hybrids with white flowers spattered red as if with blood. Better known are hybrids such as "L'arc-en-ciel" ("Rainbow") or "Grand Soleil" ("Great Sun"). The common many-flowered epiphytes most often found growing on window-sills can stand even strong sun, but most species prefer partial shade and glasshouse conditions. More delicate are the "Ackermannii" with red flowers and the "Deutsche Kaiserin" with smaller but numerous pink flowers. Other known hybrids bear white, yellow, red, orange, and bright coloured blooms. Also highly valued are plants with double flowers and dwarf plants.

Eriocactus leninghausii (HAAGE JR.) BACKBG.

The genus *Notocactus* at one time included the now independent genus *Brasilicactus*, comprising several Brazilian species with numerous small flowers, and the genus *Eriocactus*, comprising larger, columnar species occurring in South Brazil and Paraguay on the low mountain ridges rising above the pampas.

Eriocactus leninghausii, broadly spherical at first, soon becomes columnar, reaching a height of about 3 feet (1 metre). A characteristic of this species is that it makes side shoots freely at the base comparatively early. The stem measures about 4 inches (10 centimetres) in diameter (this hardly ever being attained in cultivation), and terminates in an oblique crown. The ribs, some thirty or more, are low and narrow. The thickly set small areoles each bear fifteen whitish-yellow spines, $\frac{1}{5}$ inch (5 millimetres) long. The central spines are bristly, the same as the radial ones, up to $1\frac{1}{2}$ inches (4 centimetres) long, a lovely golden-yellow, and curving towards the stem which is further covered on the crown with thick white wool. Even small seedlings are covered with the golden spines. Older specimens bear a large number of yellow flowers on the crown 2 inches (5 centimetres) long and 2 inches (5 centimetres) wide. The plant has an abundance of delicate brown seeds which have good powers of germination. *E. leninghausii* is a very handsome cactus popular with growers and highly prized by commercial dealers.

The seeds sometimes produce dwarf seedlings (the so-called *apelii* form) which have stunted roots and thick, shorter and darker spines. They make side shoots freely at a very early stage. Like forms may occur in other species as well. It seems that this phenomenon is not unknown in many other genera, for example in the case of globose species one may find columnar specimens differing from the normal plant by smaller flowers and fewer seeds.

Espostoa lanata (HBK) BR. et R.

White-haired Cerei are decorative and striking cacti. The characteristic North American representative of this group is the "Old Man", *Cephalocereus senilis*, growing in the hot ravines of the Mexican plateau, the best known being the "Valley of Old Men" near the village of Venados. The South American Andes are the home of a number of hairy cerei, belonging to several genera. *Espostoa lanata*, discovered by the famous Humboldt, however, is and will remain the most memorable of them all. The original type form, growing in Huanabamba in Northern Peru, was sought by botanists and travellers, including the well-known Roezl, for decades (Humboldt discovered it before 1823 and Roezl collected it again in about 1869).

The true *Espostoa lanata* forms branched columns and bushes of stems attaining a height of about 13 feet (4 metres) in the wild. The stems, covered with twenty to thirty low ribs, measure about 8 inches (20 centimetres) in diameter. The densely set areoles bear long white hairs which envelop the plant and give it its peculiar attraction. The many radial spines are yellow with reddish tips. The inch-long central spines, usually two in number, are quite thick, yellow, with brownish-red tips. The flowers arise from the thick white wool of the cephalium which grows from the axis on the crown and extends in a vertical groove about 5 feet (1.5 metres) down one side of the stem. The white to pink flowers are $2\frac{1}{2}$—3 inches (6—7 centimetres) long, the seeds are carmine.

The years have yielded numerous varieties and geographical forms of which many can be considered natural hybrids.

In collections *lanata* seedlings are usually grafted on short, strong stock. They are a showpiece of any collection even though specimens grown in Europe do not produce flowers.

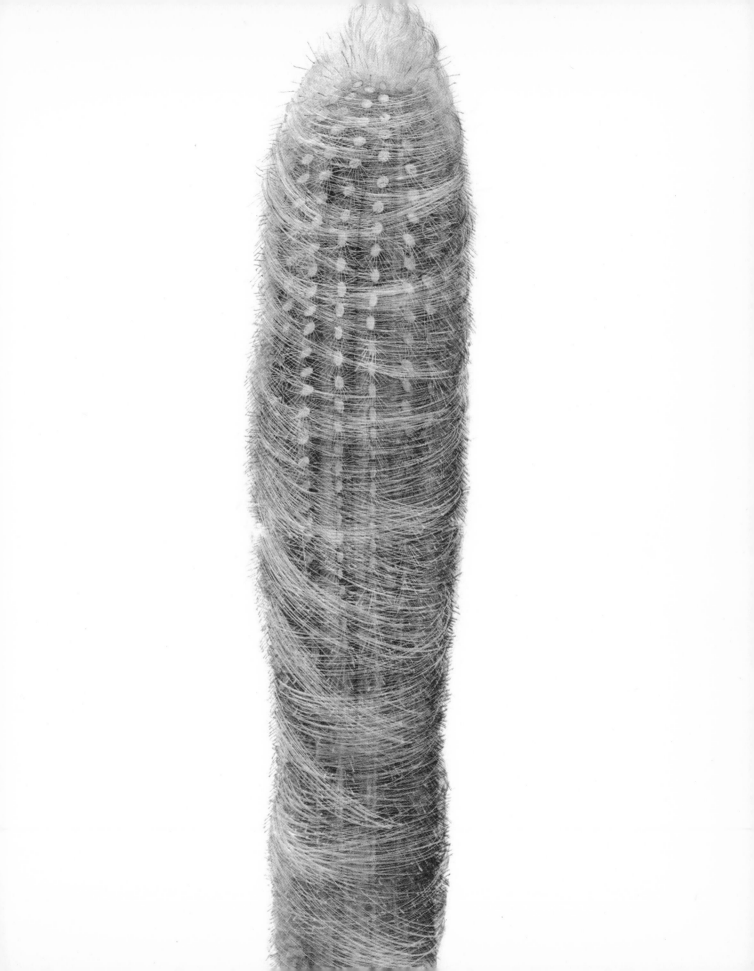

Gymnocalycium baldianum SPEG.

The genus *Gymnocalycium* includes characteristic South American cacti that are perhaps the most popular of all with growers. Collectors find them attractive for their variety of shape, ribs, spines, flowers and seeds, whereas cultivators appreciate their ease of culture and wealth of flowers, often blooming the whole day long. The reason is that in their native habitat the climate is mild and moist and they grow in partial shade so that they easily adapt to conditions in Europe.

Gymnocalycium baldianum was described in 1905 by the Argentinian botanist Spegazzini. The stem of this cactus is spherical, somewhat flattened, and coloured blue-grey. The areoles bear five to seven almost straight radial spines. The flowers arise on the crown, open wide in sunlight and are coloured purple. As most of the *Gymnocalycium* bear white, pink or yellow flowers the dark red blooms of *G. baldianum* caused a sensation among cactus growers.

Cultivation is easy. Like all gymnocalycia this species does not tolerate long periods of sun or a permanently dry environment during the growth period. In winter, on the other hand, it requires a dry and cool atmosphere. Propagation is best from the seed.

Gymnocalycium friedrichii (WERD.) PAŽ, (*G. michanovichii* var. *friedrichii*)

Gymnocalycium friedrichii is native to Bolivia where it was discovered in 1935 by A. M. Friedrich. It is a small plant, about 2½ inches (6 centimetres) high, with a rough-textured brownish-red skin. Even young specimens have buds throughout the summer which develop into pink blossoms in uncommonly large numbers.

G. friedrichii does not tolerate strong sun and it is recommended that the plant be grafted. It does well in soil with humus and requires regular substantial watering.

Today it is more numerous in European, American and Japanese collections than in its native Bolivian habitat.

44

Gymnocalycium denudatum (LK. et OTTO) PFEIFF.

Gymnocalycia have long been known in European collections (the first specimens of this genus have been known for almost 150 years), yet their true wealth was discovered only recently by modern growers. Despite their great variety many original species are in danger of becoming extinct as a result of soil cultivation and the advance of civilization in their native land, mainly in Argentina and Uruguay, and also because of their great popularity.

Gymnocalycium denudatum (*denudatus* means naked) has been known for more than a hundred years and has remained one of the basic species of every collection. In 1825 the original plants were sent by Sellow from southern Brazil or Uruguay to Berlin where three years later they were given the name of *Echinocactus denudatus*. The stem is globose or slightly columnar, up to 4 inches (10 centimetres) across and 8 inches (20 centimetres) high in age, making side shoots freely from the base. The skin is a glossy pale green. The ribs, numbering five to eight, are divided by faint cross grooves. The large, pale brown, felted areoles have five light brown, appressed, slightly curved spines, about ¾ inch (1.5 centimetres) long. The flowers arise near the crown, are pure white, sometimes tinged with pink.

Today collectors cultivate two types of *G. denudatum*, namely the so-called German type described above and a second type brought by C. Backeberg from southern Brazil. Both are lovely and flower profusely throughout the summer. They should be sheltered from direct sun and grown in rich porous soil. During the growing period they require more water. Propagation is from the seed or from shoots detached from older plants.

46

Gymnocalycium denudatum cv. "jan šuba" paž.

In discussing gymnocalycia or cacti as such it is necessary to warn growers against chance or intentional hybridization of these plants, for cactus growing should primarily be concerned with the collecting and cultivation of natural, so-called wild species, varieties and forms. In some countries, however, especially in America and Japan, great attention is also devoted (in botany as well) to cactus hybrids, the object of interest to gardeners and cultivators in Europe for years past. It will therefore not be amiss if we make an exception and include here amidst the spherical cacti at least one such hybrid which can truly be considered a worthwhile specimen.

The plant in question is a cross between two different species of *Gymnocalycium* — *G. denudatum* var. *backebergii* and *G. baldianum*. The hybrid was named by its creator Dr. Pažout after the successful Czech cactus grower Jan Šuba. From one of its parents this cactus has inherited its nice, glossy green stem, the size and colour of the blossoms and the size of the seeds, whereas the other endowed it with great hardiness and proliferous, brightly coloured flowers. "Jan Šuba" is thus a hybrid in which the growers succeeded in combining the advantageous traits of both parents and in assuring their continued propagation. During the twenty-five years following the creation of this hybrid the growers have succeeded to a certain extent in gaining uniform offspring grown from the seed. The plant is self-pollinating and the germinating seed produces uniform seedlings resembling the parent plant *G. denudatum* var. *backebergii*. These soon bear frequent, large flowers coloured pink to carmine with pollen-bearing anthers and a fully developed stigma.

Leuchtenbergia principis HOOK.

Among the many remarkable Mexican cacti one that heads the list is *Leuchtenbergia principis*, chiefly for its bizarre shape which is more like a small agave than a cactus. The strong, turnip-like root bears long, slender, triangular tubercles, up to 6 inches (15 centimetres) long in adult specimens, terminated by long, straw-coloured spines. The spines are flat, soft, blunt, often interlaced, the one or two central spines attaining a length of 6 inches (15 centimetres). The flowers, arising on the youngest tubercles, are fragrant, yellow, about 3 inches (8 centimetres) across. They open in sunlight and last several days.

In its native habitat of San Luis Potosí and Hidalgo, it grows scattered over a fairly large territory amidst grass and small agaves up to an elevation of 6,500 feet (2,000 metres). It is no wonder, then, that these plants were collected in all sizes by the thousand. The largest ever found measured 20—28 inches (50—70 centimetres) in height.

L. principis was named in honour of Duke Leuchtenberg, Napoleon's brother-in-law; the specific name *principis* means princely. It belongs to the genus *Leuchtenbergia* of which it is the only member.

L. principis is a hardy, undemanding plant, well suited for cultivation on the window-sill provided it has sufficient light and warmth. It does not tolerate direct sun and should be planted in heavier, rich and porous, clay soil. Propagation is from the seed. The first few days after germination the seedlings are very delicate and in later years have a slow growth, like all plants which have their own roots. To accelerate growth they are grafted on short stock of *Eriocereus jusbertii*, on which they grow and flower rapidly.

50

Lobivia famatimensis (SPEG.) BACKBG.

Years ago the Argentinian botanist Spegazzini described an unusual and interesting cactus from the Andean volcanic massif Famatina and named this small cactus with turnip-like root and yellow flowers, growing at an elevation of 6,500—10,000 feet (2,000—3,000 metres), *Lobivia famatimensis*. Little did he know that it would one day become the subject of controversy amongst experts, a controversy that still remains unresolved. This cactus was originally discovered in 1873 by two German botanists and later made its way under the name of *Echinocactus reichii* to all collections where it was a great favourite for its peculiar stem, covered with miniature tubercles with small appressed spines.

The controversy was provoked in the 1930s by the traveller and cactus dealer Backeberg when he declared quite different plants which he found in another Argentine province to be *Lobivia famatimensis*. His error was pointed out by A. V. Frič. In 1935 Harry Blossfeld searched for the true *L. famatimensis* but in vain. Not till 1955 did F. Ritter find the plant discovered by Spegazzini on the slopes of Famatina; however, Backeberg refused to acknowledge that this was a lobivia to the end of his days. In the meantime Backeberg's *L. famatimensis* became a stand-by of almost every collection, popular with growers for its brightly coloured flowers, ranging from yellow to red in all shades, sometimes even white. They are known under various names (*L. pectinifera, Hymenorebutia*, etc.).

All these *Lobivia* "*famatimensis*" are distributed over a wide range where they occur as mountain cacti. In cultivation they bear proliferous flowers in a wide range of colours at the beginning of summer. They are a source of great pleasure to cactus growers, especially when cultivated in the open, without glass, in mountain air.

Lobivia jajoiana BACKBG.

Prior to World War I cactus growers knew only a few species of the large genus *Lobivia*, classing them under the genus *Echinopsis*. It was not until after the war that the renewed interest in cactus growing opened to collectors the great wealth of mountain and alpine locations. The habitat of the small, hardy lobivias is Bolivia (which also gave its name to the genus), north-west Argentina and partly also Peru.

In the province of Salta in north-west Argentina at an elevation of 10,000 feet (3,000 metres) grows one of the loveliest of all lobivias named by C. Backeberg after the Brno cactus grower and painter G. Jája. The stem, as a rule, is globose, later columnar, up to 4 inches (10 centimetres) high, glossy, dark green, with twelve to fourteen ribs divided into slanting tubercles. The spines are pale to black-brown in youth, the eight to ten radial spines measuring $\frac{1}{2}$ inch (1 centimetre) in length. The one to three central spines are stronger, dark, frequently red, the upper spine attains a length of $1\frac{1}{4}$ inches (3 centimetres) and is hooked. The flowers are $2\frac{1}{2}$ inches (6.5 centimetres) across, tomato red with dark purple throat, thickened at the edge and glossy.

This lovely species is a good choice for modest circumstances. It thrives wherever there is plenty of sun and fresh air in summer, mainly in the country, which has none of the polluted air of the cities. Grown on its own roots it does well in heavier, porous and nourishing soil. In winter it requires a light, dry environment with a temperature of 6—8°C (43—46°F). Propagation is easy from the seed.

Lophophora williamsii (LEM. ex SD.) COULT.

No book, handbook or treatise on cacti omits to mention the strange Mexican cactus worshipped by the Indians and providing them with a potent narcotic. Already in 1790 it was given the name *Peyotl zacatensis*, today known as *Lophophora*.

Lophophoras are small, grey-green or yellow-green cacti with a soft, rubbery stem and strong turnip-like root. The areoles bear tufts of white wool. The small, frequent flowers arise from the wool on the crown and are generally coloured pinkish violet, white, or yellow. The soft pink fruit contains numerous black seeds. Some varieties form whole groups of stems and cristate forms are likewise not uncommon. Their habitat is central and northern Mexico, where some districts and villages even bear the plant's Indian name, for example Lomerias de Peyote, Peyotán, or San Jésus Pyotl, pyotl being of Aztec or even earlier origin.

Lophophora williamsii and related cacti were used by Indians for the preparation of a narcotic, the alkaloids contained in the plant producing colour and sound hallucinations. Dried plants later became a lucrative business and whole tribes, especially from the north, journeyed to the southern United States and Mexico to collect these cacti. The ceremonies at which these narcotics were used (originally religious cult ceremonies) were soon prohibited and in their stead a special church worshipping these plants was founded in the United States, the faithful receiving them as the Host. Much has been written in scientific literature about the effects of peyote usage, and research on these cacti is of interest even to those who are not cactus growers.

Growers, however, will appreciate the hardiness of these plants. They withstand even the hottest sun in summer, the air of big cities, dry and heavy soil just as ample watering and rich, porous soil. In winter, however, they prefer to be left undisturbed in a dry, cold atmosphere. They are true examples of the proverbial hardiness of cacti.

56

Mammillaria bombycina QUEHL.

Most mammillarias come from Mexico. Characteristic of these plants are the conical to cylindrical nipples called mammillae which cover the stem, instead of the usual ribs, and the wreaths of small flowers growing from their axils. After the flowering period the wool in these axils is an attractive foil for the decorative fruit. This fruit is edible, often very tasty, and the Mexicans gather it much like the Europeans gather forest berries. The large genus of *Mammillaria* differs from the other cacti not only in the great variety of species (several hundred), but also in their delicate beauty and easy cultivation.

One of the better known species growing freely in large clumps is *M. bombycina*. Its lovely spines make it an attractive plant even when not in flower. Besides the many white radial spines it bears central spines that are coloured brown to red, creating a glowing contrast against the white felted areoles. The lower spines are longer and hooked. The flowers, arranged in a wreath on the crown, are greenish-red outside, pink-red inside with darker stripes. The individual stems are about $2\frac{1}{2}$ inches (6 centimetres) across and attain a height of up to 8 inches (20 centimetres). As one can see, this is a fairly robust species, especially when the older specimens spread to form clumps. The colourfulness of this cactus is most striking when viewed at close range or on a good coloured microfilm which reveals the true beauty of the spines.

The home of this species is Coahuila, Mexico. Although comparatively abundant in the wild it is better to cultivate it from the seed contained in the whitish, club-shaped fruit, thus giving the cultivator the opportunity to observe its development from seedling to full grown adult — one of the most interesting aspects of cactus growing. Besides, this will also help preserve the beauty of the Mexican countryside. The number of these lovely plants has rapidly diminished and there is grave danger of their complete extinction should large-scale collecting continue.

Mammillaria centricirrha LEM.

Mammillaria centricirrha, along with *M. pusilla* and *M. bocasana*, is one of the commonest Mexican cacti. It has been cultivated for more than a hundred years and numerous varieties and forms have been described in the literature, some, alas, of hybrid origin. Craig lists more than 116 synonyms, more than half of them as varieties of *M. centricirrha*. It is a dark green, globose, later columnar plant up to 12 inches (30 centimetres) high and 4 inches (10 centimetres) across. The nipples are angular, arranged in spiralled rows. The radial spines, four or five, are about ¾ inch (2 centimetres) long. The one or two central spines are a pale colour with dark tip, curved. The flowers form a wreath at the top. They are about 1 inch (2.5 centimetres) across, pale pink with a darker central stripe.

The best known varieties are *bockii*, *divergens*, *recurva*, and *krameri* described by K. Schumann. *M. centricirrha* is popular, especially with beginners, for its easy cultivation and proliferous flowers which appear from May to June.

It requires a heavier, rich, porous soil, light, heat and sufficient moisture during the growing period. In winter a light, dry environment and temperature of 8°C (46°F). Propagation is usually from the seed, the seedlings already bearing flowers in the third year. Growers will welcome the fact that mammillarias, particularly the hardiest species, do not need to be grafted.

Mammillaria hahniana WERD.

What makes mammillarias so attractive is the bright colouring of the flowers and the colourfulness of the stems, or rather of the dense spines covering the whole plant which may be white, yellow, brown to red or dark. The colours of some species sometimes differ in the varieties or geographical forms. Thus, for instance, the well-known *Mammillaria rhodantha* embraces a whole range of hues, the loveliest forms being those which glow with reddish tints in the sun when sprinkled with water. The most popular species, however, are the white ones, of which there are a great number. In many instances the colour of the spines is reflected in the name of the species, as for example *M. candida*, *M. roseoalba*, *M. albilanata*, etc. *M. hahniana* is one of the white species distinguished, moreover, by fine hairs.

Mammillaria hahniana forms large clumps of heads and is known for the great variability of its spines, both in length and in density. The loveliest are the forms with long white hairs completely covering the stems, which are pale green and only about 4 inches (10 centimetres) in diameter. The clumps of heads are quite large in their native habitat (Mexico, Guanachuato and Querétaro). This species has a milky juice, stems covered with closely set nipples, and axils bearing short white wool and a large number of spines. The great majority of these spines change into fine hairs, up to $1\frac{1}{2}$ inches (4 centimetres) or more in length, completely enveloping the stem and giving the plant its characteristic look. The small flowers appearing in June are about $\frac{1}{2}$—$\frac{3}{4}$ inch (1—2 centimetres) across and coloured purplish-red inside. The fruit is also red, about $\frac{1}{4}$ inch (7 millimetres) long, and contains large, $\frac{1}{12}$ inch (1.5 millimetres), brown seeds.

Mammillaria sheldonii (BR. et R.) BÖD.

Mammillarias are modest cacti, as a rule, which can be cultivated with ease even though some species are more delicate and require greater care. Almost all like a moist sunny situation without being subjected to a scorching sun in the growing period. In winter they require a cool — about 5—10°C (41—50°F) — and dry atmosphere. Propagation is from shoots or from the seed.

They are not distinguished by unusual or robust shapes, sharp spines or large flowers, but they are a must in every collection for their colour as well as their gay and at the same time calming effect.

Most mammillarias have spherical, club-shaped to cylindrical stems and many make side shoots or twin stems, thus forming large clumps of heads, especially in their native habitat. *Mammillaria sheldonii* which grows most abundantly in Sonora, Mexico, has elongate stems up to 10 inches (25 centimetres) long, and about $2\frac{1}{2}$ inches (6 centimetres) in diameter, which make side shoots at the base. The not too lengthy spines are whitish with brownish-red tips. The central spines are thicker and darker, the lower one is hooked. The flowers are about $\frac{3}{4}$—1 inch (2—3 centimetres) broad, greenish-brown outside and pink inside. The club-shaped fruit is red, the seed black.

M. sheldonii requires heavier, porous soil and plenty of light and heat during the growing period. It does not tolerate continual damp.

Mammillaria zeilmanniana BÖD.

Because of the vast number of species, mammillarias have been divided by growers and scientists into several sections or groups with the same or like characteristics. *Mammillaria zeilmanniana* belongs to the group of fleshy species with roots that do not tolerate continual damp. It was discovered in 1931 by E. Georgi of Saltilla growing in stony ground. Its native habitat is Mexico — Guanajuato, near San Miguel Allende.

The stem is small, round or cylindrical, about $2\frac{1}{2}$ inches (6 centimetres) high and 2 inches (4.5 centimetres) across. The colour is dark green. The nipples are dense, ovoid or cylindrical and are terminated by areoles with fifteen to eighteen radiating thin white spines. The four central spines are reddish brown; three of these are straight whereas the lowest is longer and hooked. The flowers appear near the crown in the form of a wreath, are violet-red or purple, about $\frac{3}{4}$ inch (2 centimetres) across.

M. zeilmanniana is one of the most floriferous species. Cultivation is the same as for all fleshy, hooked, clump-forming mammillarias. During the growing period it requires adequate sunlight, heat and moisture. In winter a dry atmosphere, light and a temperature of 8—10°C (46—50°F). Propagation is usually from the seed.

The specific name *zeilmanniana* is after H. Zeilmann, member of the German Cactus Society.

66

Notocactus concinnus (MONV.) BERG.

The genus *Notocactus*, established as a sub-genus of *Echinocactus* in 1898 by Schumann, has undergone many changes since then. Today it comprises only part of the original number of notocacti which are very popular with growers. In the main these are small plants growing freely in the grassy pampas of South America or beneath thin shrubs which protect them from the scorching sun and from becoming too dry. In collections they likewise do not like excessive heat or a scorching sun and during the growing period require ample watering. Marked alkalinity of the soil is not beneficent either.

Notocacti grow well from the seed and the young plants need not be grafted. Old specimens, however, lose their roots easily and take root again with difficulty. They grow better on short stock, on which they also flower more profusely. Even fairly small seedlings bear the glowing yellow flowers with purple stigmas. These plants are particularly suitable for beginners for learning how to care for South American species and how to grow like plants from the seed. It is a pity that in age some notocacti become columnar, their stems lose their firmness and nice shape and turn grey and woody at the base.

The small *Notocactus concinnus*, which forms groups of low heads, comes from southern Brazil and Uruguay. Characteristic of this species is the spineless crown. The individual stems measure 2—4 inches (5—10 centimetres) with about eighteen ribs covered with short pale yellow bristles. The central spines, about $\frac{1}{5}$—$\frac{3}{5}$ inch (4—15 millimetres) long, are set crosswise and coloured dark to pale brown. The flowers are profuse, 2—2$\frac{1}{2}$ inches (5—7 centimetres) broad, glowing yellow, tinged with red on the outside. The buds and flower tube are covered with whitish wool and brownish bristles.

This species is often mistaken for *N. apricus*, which has spines on the crown, is usually bigger and always solitary.

68

Obregonia denegrii FRIČ

This small cactus was discovered in 1923 by A. V. Frič and Ing. Marecelino Castanedo on their journey through the calciferous desert in Lanos del Joumave, when their car broke down. While his friends were making the necessary repairs Frič scouted around in the vicinity and found there a number of interesting plants including *Obregonia denegrii*. Of this event he writes: "*Obregonia denegrii* is a truly rare plant. My three-day search of the desert yielded only three hundred specimens. I have named the plant after the Mexican president Alvaro Obregon, for whom I have the highest esteem and who has won the respect and love of the Mexican people." The specific name is after the Mexican Minister of Agriculture Denegri.

O. denegrii resembles the artichoke. The stem grows to 4 inches (10 centimetres) in diameter, is low, coloured green and terminates in a strong turnip-like root. The triangular, comparatively short tubercles are spirally arranged. The areoles at the tips are covered with white felt and bear two to four yellowish spines. The flowers arise from the youngest areoles, are whitish or cream-coloured and measure about ¾ inch (2 centimetres) across. The fruit grows inside the stem and when ripe the soft white berry appears in the thick white wool.

Although it is a rare plant whose export has been prohibited by the Mexican government, several thousand specimens were shipped to Europe on more than one occasion. The imported plants differ from seedlings both in the shape and colour of the stem, which is more grey-green with a pink tinge and has a strong turnip-like root. Seedlings are best grown grafted on short *Echinopsis* stock. They are a fresh green, do not tolerate direct sunlight and grow well from the seed. Imported specimens should be planted in porous, clay soil and watered with care. In winter they require light and a temperature of 10—12°C (50—54°F). Water is applied only to grafted plants.

Opuntia microdasys (LEHM.) PFEIFF.

For most people the word cactus calls to mind the *Opuntia*, probably because this large genus comprises the greatest number of species of varied sizes and shapes and also because it grows practically all over the world. Soon after the discovery of the American continent, opuntias spread to Spain and the whole Mediterranean region, including North Africa and the Near East. They were also introduced into other, sometimes very distant, countries such as Australia, where they became so widespread that they became a menace to agricultural crops. Opuntias have a remarkably rapid rate of multiplication; under favourable circumstances the smallest joint or even part of a joint can grow roots in any position and survive even such unfavourable conditions as drought, heat and sometimes frost. Frost-resistant species are to be found as far north as Canada, where they must survive long harsh winters with much snow, and *Opuntia vulgaris* grows in the wild in the southern Tyrol. Opuntias have become the symbol of all cacti and are even part of the state coat-of-arms in Mexico. They are also abundant in South America. In the Andes they are the only taller plants to have penetrated as far as the edge of the glaciers where groups of white *Tephrocactus* look like snow fields or flocks of sheep from a distance.

Cactus growers do not include the common opuntias in their collections because they take up a large amount of space and because it is necessary to handle them with care so that the skin of the hands does not come in contact with the glochids which cause unpleasant itching. On the other hand there are many species that are small and interesting or unusually decorative. One of these is *O. microdasys*, a truly striking cactus. It makes low, thick clumps and its greatest attraction is the closely set cushions of glochids growing from spineless areoles. In the type plant they are a bright yellow, in var. *rufida* brown to brownish-red, and in var. *albispina* white. Other noteworthy varieties of this popular species are the dwarf var. *laevior* and *undulata* hort., distinguished by wavy joints.

Parodia mutabilis BACKBG.

This species was discovered and described by Frič's pupil C. Backeberg, globe-trotter and collector of cacti as well as author of the most extensive monograph and many other books on the subject.

The native habitat of this cactus is the warm, wine-growing province of Salta, a magic spot in the Andes foothills. *Parodia mutabilis* has a spherical fleshy stem, 3 inches (8 centimetres) across at the most. As in most members of this genus the many ribs are spirally arranged and divided into low tubercles. The radial spines are numerous (up to fifty to each areole) white, delicate bristles. The four stronger central spines are about $\frac{2}{5}$—$\frac{3}{5}$ inch (1—1.5 centimetres) long, orange-brown to red. The many hairy buds on the crown open into small flowers 1—2 inches (3—5 centimetres) broad, coloured whitish-yellow to yellow. *P. mutabilis* is easy to cultivate and has three different varieties.

P. mutabilis var. *carneospina* has larger tubercles and a crown covered with white wool. The central spines are pale brown to meaty red with a darker tip. *P. mutabilis* var. *elegans* differs from the type plant mainly in that the spines and entire habit are finer and more delicate. *P. mutabilis* var. *ferruginea* has rust-coloured spines.

These varieties are thus classified for the purpose of recording the characteristic aberrations of these plants, collected, as a rule, on different sites where the offspring likewise retain the distinguishing traits. These characteristics are permanent even in the case of adult plants grown from the seed sown in Europe. In its native habitat, however, *Parodia* is a very variable genus, still in the stage of evolution. It is thus questionable whether there is any point in distinguishing so many different varieties and sometimes species when many were created chiefly as a result of personal interest or for commercial reasons.

74

Parodia sanguiniflora FRIČ EX BACKBG.

The cacti which Spegazzini classed in a separate genus called after the botanist Parodi have not been known long. Only about three species had been described prior to World War I. The first flood of new plants, launched by A. V. Frič and lasting to this day, dates from the 1920s. Today there are one hundred known species of this beautiful genus. Its native habitat is the mountains of north-west Argentina and neighbouring Bolivia and broad parts of Paraguay as well as south and central Brazil.

Parodia sanguiniflora is one of the first and most valuable precious plants discovered by A. V. Frič, who thought highly of this and other parodias, writing of collecting them in the following words:

"It was my lucky day, the kind that comes once in a blue moon. The weather was foul — it was raining, the wind buffeted us on the ridges of the sharp cliffs and we had to hurry because dusk was falling and we didn't want the storm and darkness to catch us in the mountains. Several *Microspermia* still had red flowers and I quickly picked them and put them in my knapsack. Growing alongside them were clumps of *Echinopsis* and unattractive *Gymnocalycium*. As I was preparing to climb down from the mountains I found flowering specimens of both, and all had red blossoms. They were the loveliest of all my finds: *Chamaecereus grandiflorus* and *Gymnocalycium venturii*. Truly one of those days which are few and far between in the life of a collector."

Parodia sanguiniflora belongs to the group of parodias with a hooked central spine and small stem measuring about 2 inches (5 centimetres) across. The many ribs are divided into spirally arranged tubercles. The radial spines are bristly and only $\frac{1}{4}$—$\frac{1}{3}$ inch (6—8 millimetres) long. The brown central spines are much stronger, sometimes more than $\frac{3}{4}$ inch (2 centimetres) long, hooked and arranged crosswise. The blood-red flowers, appearing in great numbers at the beginning of summer in cultivation, arise from the crown. Most parodias grow well on their own roots and cultivation is easy. They are very rewarding plants.

Pseudolobivia aurea (BR. et R.) BACKBG.

The genus *Pseudolobivia* comprises South American cacti which, according to Backeberg, represent a transition between *Echinopsis* with its striking nocturnal blooms with long tubes and *Lobivia* with its brightly coloured, diurnal flowers with shorter tubes. The classification of cacti into these genera has been the subject of a controversy which to this day has not been brought to a satisfactory conclusion. We, however, shall adhere to the terminology defended by Backeberg in his extensive monograph, and for practical growers it will suffice to supplement the illustration with some brief information about the plant.

Pseudolobivia aurea is a lovely, hardy cactus that does not attain large dimensions. It is popular with growers for its large yellow flowers which appear frequently and with regularity. The Sierra Chica mountains near Cordoba, Argentina, where these plants originate, have a climate not unlike ours. The stem of this cactus, dubbed the "Star of Cordoba" by the natives, resembles that of the echinopses that bear large white nocturnal flowers — in other words it is not particularly striking and grows to only about 4 inches (10 centimetres) in diameter. However, when the plant bears hairy buds (this is nothing out of the ordinary in a sunny situation) which subsequently develop into beautiful flowers 4 inches (10 centimetres) long and 3 inches (8 centimetres) wide, coloured lemon to golden yellow it is indeed a splendid sight to behold, for they really seem to glow like stars.

Besides the type plant which was first discovered at an elevation of 3,500 feet (1,000 metres) there are several varieties, evidence that these cacti are distributed over a fairly wide range.

Pseudolobivia kermesina KRAINZ

When the first red *Pseudolobivia* was described in the trying days of World War II it did not cause the sensation aroused by the discovery of the first red *Gymnocalycium*. The popularity of cacti was already on the wane at that time and besides cactus growers were somewhat sceptical towards echinopsis-like plants, for hybrids were not uncommon among them.

It was not until after the war that this lovely and rewarding new cactus came into its own — an object of admiration and a welcome addition to every collection. Most of the other species of this genus have attractive flowers but all are white, except for *Pseudolobivia aurea* which has yellow blossoms.

Pseudolobivia kermesina is a fairly large plant and in cultivation its stem may grow to more than 6 inches (15 centimetres) in diameter. The skin is a fresh green, lighter than in any other *Pseudolobivia*, sometimes even yellow-green. The fifteen to twenty-three ribs are divided by marked grooves. Each areole bears some ten to fifteen radial spines which are up to about ½ inch (15 millimetres) long, yellow with brown tips, later becoming grey. The five central spines are of like colour but longer — up to 1 inch (3 centimetres) long. All are fairly thin, needle-like and sharp. The flowers, about 7 inches (18 centimetres) long and sometimes up to 4 inches (10 centimetres) across, are carmine-red inside and last about three days. In cultivation some plants have been known to bear flowers which do not open fully, sometimes remaining completely closed and wilting after having put out only the end of the pistil and stigma. Large adult plants provided with the necessary requirements for good growth (rich soil, heat and light) bear flowers in profusion. I have had the opportunity to observe plants which have produced up to ten blossoms at one time. *P. kermesina* is without doubt the loveliest species of this genus and is a must in every collection. It probably comes from Argentina but its exact location is not known.

Rebutia senilis BACKBG.

The genera *Lobivia*, *Mediolobivia*, *Aylostera* and *Rebutia* form the nucleus of the wealth of small, high-mountain, brightly coloured South American cacti discovered in the period between the two World Wars when cactus growing was at the height of its popularity. The most attractive feature of these cacti is the spring beauty and silky sheen of the flowers and their incomparable wealth of colour. If one wants to turn a person into an avid cactus grower the best way is to make him a gift of the small *R. miniscula* in springtime with its red grains of the blooms to be, for then he is certain to succumb.

A few words now about another, newer species of *Rebutia* which Backeberg brought to Europe in 1932 and named *Rebutia senilis* because of its long white spines. It is a fairly robust species with the low spherical stem measuring up to 3 inches (8 centimetres) in height. The dark green skin is covered with a thick coat of bristly spines up to 1 inch (3 centimetres) long, almost completely concealing the plant. The ribs are in the form of tubercles. In all the *Rebutia* the blossoms arise from the lower areoles but in this species they may appear higher up. The flower is $1\frac{1}{2}$ inches (3.5 centimetres) broad, carmine-red with white throat and pointed petals. The fruit is yellow-orange. In its native habitat near Salta in north-west Argentina *R. senilis* occurs in many varieties, differing from the type plant chiefly in the spines, colour and size of the flowers. Conditions for growing this cactus are the same as for all members of the genus. Rebutias do best in porous soil in low boxes or tins, should be transplanted in August and kept in a cold, 0—5°C (32—41°F), dry environment during the winter. The flowering is followed by a dormant period which lasts until September.

Strombocactus disciformis (DC) BR. et R.

Mexico is not only a country of extinct Indian cultures but also the home of the relics of old genera of cacti of which all that remains today are several isolated and interesting groups. These include the genera *Lophophora, Aztekium, Obregonia, Astrophytum, Thelocactus, Turbinicarpus* and the monogenus *Strombocactus*. These are and always will be rare plants and although under government protection many are in danger of becoming extinct, thanks to the interest of commercial dealers.

Some of these cacti are shown here on this and the following pages. *Strombocactus disciformis* is one. It grows in the crevices of steep cliffs near Mineral del Monte, Hidalgo, in central Mexico. Even here it is a comparatively rare plant. In the wild it is said to attain a height of 3 inches (8 centimetres) and diameter of 7 inches (18 centimetres). In Europe, however, such a large specimen is unknown and cactus growers must be satisfied with much smaller plants. The body, rising from a turnip-like root, is hard, pale grey-green, and covered with closely set tubercles. The crown is topped with sparse grey-white wool and delicate spines that are not very long and soon disappear. The flowers emerging on the crown are $\frac{3}{4}$—$1\frac{1}{2}$ inches (2—4 centimetres) broad and cream-coloured tinged with yellow. The dry fruit conceals a very small brown seed which previously proved difficult to grow. Today the seed is sown in sterilized substrata in hermetically sealed jars and the seedlings are grafted on to *Peireskia* or *Echinopsis*. This makes propagation easier, but even so these cacti continue to be rare plants that are much in demand.

84

Thelocactus bicolor (GAL.) BR. et R.

The genus *Thelocactus* today comprises only those Mexican species formerly belonging to *Echinocactus* which have a broadly funnel-shaped flower with short, scaly tube. The ribs are generally divided by grooves or in the form of tubercles, the spines straight and dry, the fruit dehiscing on the under side, the seed black. Of interest to cactus growers is the fact that this genus includes numerous cultivated species. *Thelocactus bicolor* is one of the most rewarding of the many that used to be imported and cultivated in great numbers but were later ousted by the influx of South American species so that, as a result, nowadays one will rarely find a complete collection of *Thelocactus*. Their beauty and variety as well as lovely flowers make these forgotten plants a welcome addition to any collection and they certainly should not be passed over in favour of rare and delicate miniatures or striking large species. The genus includes some twenty different species so that there is no difficulty in acquiring a complete collection. True, some species and varieties may be hard to come by but this should prove a challenge to the cactus grower to try and acquire them all and thus preserve this bit of the fast-disappearing Mexico at least in collections.

T. bicolor is a comparatively small, globose cactus with eight prominent ribs, purplish-pink flowers and attractive spines growing from the closely set areoles. Each bears up to eighteen radial spines and four strong, central spines coloured yellow to red. The open flower sometimes measures more than 2 inches (5 centimetres) across. The fruit is fairly small, about $\frac{1}{2}$ inch (1 centimetre) and the seed is large with good powers of germination.

Turbinicarpus lophophoroides (WERD.) BUXB. et BACKBG.

The cacti of the genus *Turbinicarpus* are among the most rewarding of Mexican dwarf cacti. Today there are only about ten known species in existence so that the cactus grower can accommodate the whole lot in one bowl. They are hard, undemanding plants that do well even without grafting. Grafting, though it promotes more rapid growth and a greater wealth of flowers, deprives the plant of its characteristic feature, namely the turnip-like root without which such plants are incomplete and without botanical value.

Turbinicarpus lophophoroides was so named because of its resemblance to the narcotic *Lophophora williamsii*. It is distinguished not only by continual flowering throughout the summer months but also by the beauty and size of the blossoms, far outshining that of the other species. It is a somewhat delicate representative of the genus and it is therefore wise to make an exception in this case and graft it on short stock. The resulting wealth of large, pink-tinged blossoms is more than worth it, even though the stem, normally about 1½ inches (3.5—4 centimetres) high, tends to be bigger and longer. The body is pale green to grey-green whereas in the other species it is darker. The ribs are divided into low tubercles. The spines are fairly short and sharp. The other species have longer, softer spines. The crown is covered with thick white felt, one of the most attractive features of this plant, from which emerge the large, silky, glossy flowers, up to 1½ inches (4 centimetres) across, found only in this species. The dark tips of the slightly curving spines are another distinguishing feature that differentiates this plant from the others. All together these distinctive features lead one to doubt whether this cactus is rightly classified as a member of the genus *Turbinicarpus*.

Zygocactus truncatus (HAW.) K. SCH.

Zygocactus truncatus and its hybrids are among the best known and commonly cultivated house plants, grown more often on the window-sills of country houses than in collections of cacti. Zygocacti, classed in Europe under the generic name of *Epiphyllum* until recently, are branching epiphytic cacti of the rain forests bearing flowers on the tips of the youngest, flat spineless joints. The blossoms appear to be double, one inside the other, with recurved petals. The plant makes shrubs, in the case of grafted specimens (usually on *Peireskia* stock) small trees with pendent crowns. These, along with *Epiphyllum* (formerly *Phyllocactus*) and sometimes *Rhipsalis*, are the most widespread epiphytic, hygrophilic cacti, generally originating in the tropical rain forests. These cacti were at one time very popular with growers who cultivated many lovely hybrids. They became common market plants and indeed are not even considered cacti by many laymen.

Zygocactus truncatus is also known as the "Christmas Cactus" because it flowers and is on sale at the end of the year when there is such a dearth of flowering plants. It forms joints about 2 inches (5 centimetres) long and $\frac{3}{4}$ inch (2 centimetres) wide and bears large, usually carmine-red flowers up to 3 inches (8 centimetres) long. During the summer it should be grown in partial shade. When the new joints have attained full growth, water should be withheld until they almost wilt; this promotes the formation of buds. Only after these appear is the plant given more water so that the flowers develop successfully. The actual period of rest follows after flowering. At this time the plant can be kept in a cooler and drier environment until spring, that is, until the new growing period.

This genus has been known in England since 1818, which year also marks the cultivation of the first hybrids. The chief merit for cultivating the greatest variety of hybrids, however, goes to the French, who have produced a wide assortment bearing white, pink, red to violet flowers from October until February.

Adromischus cristatus (HAW.) LEM.

The plants on this and the following pages are succulents which, like cacti, adapted the shape of the stem and the structure of the body to the dry and arid conditions in which they grow. Unlike the cacti, however, the reduction in body surface is not so great. As a rule the leaves are thick and filled with water, serving as the plant's reservoir, and the skin is likewise often thick and sometimes covered with a coat of wax or hairs to prevent excessive evaporation. Although these plants do not have as striking flowers as the cacti, they are just as colourful and interesting.

The genus *Adromischus* has about fifty species, most of them forming small shrubs. The leaves are flat, oval or club-shaped, sometimes with bright coloured spots. The flowers are small, whitish, tinged with red, growing in clusters and often singly as well. Most of the species are found in south or south-west Africa.

Growers cultivate several interesting species distinguished by their attractively coloured leaves, for example *A. maculatus*, forming shrubs about 4 inches (10 centimetres) high with large, rounded, fleshy leaves dotted with large red-brown spots; *A. marianae*, with a short stem and narrow, fleshy leaves covered with red-brown spots; and *A. festivus*, *A. kessleringianus*, *A. trigynus* and *A. triflorus*, perhaps the prettiest members of the genus.

Adromischus cristatus is the hardiest of them all and also the best known. It makes small clumps about 3 inches (8 centimetres) across with a short stem, which later branches and makes many aerial roots at the base. The leaves are a mat green, fleshy, ovoid, about 1½ inches (4 centimetres) long and wavy at the tip. The flower stalk is 6—8 inches (15—20 centimetres) long and bears small, green-pink flowers opening in summer. It requires a warm, sunny situation and heavier, porous soil, and in winter a temperature of 12—15°C (54—59°F). It is propagated with ease by cuttings or the leaves, which soon take root and make small plants. It also grows well from the seed.

The native habitat is Cape Province and the specific name *cristatus* means comb-like.

Agave victoriae reginae T. MOORE

The genus *Agave* contains some three hundred species which are just as distinctive succulents of the stony deserts of Mexico and Central America as the Cactaceae.

The loveliest member of this genus is *Agave victoriae reginae* of Nuevo Leon in northern Mexico. It makes thick, broadly spherical, usually stemless rosettes about 20—28 inches (50—70 centimetres) across. The leaves are angular, stiff, erect, slightly curving towards the plant's centre, about 6 inches (15 centimetres) long, 3 inches (7 centimetres) wide at the base, and tapering towards the tip. The colour is dark green, with white stripes on the sides and edges that broaden towards the tip of the leaf. The end of the leaf terminates in three black-brown spines, two small and one strong one about $\frac{3}{4}$ inch (2 centimetres) long. After many years it bears flowers on a stalk 13 feet (4 metres) high.

Some agaves are cultivated by Mexicans on plantations for their juice. The concealed bud is removed and the sweet juice is gathered daily from the cut and left to ferment in leather vats to yield the popular wine "pulque". Distillation produces the liqueur called "tequila". Use is also made of the bast fibres of the leaves, which are cut before flowering.

Agaves were introduced to Europe about 1561, becoming domesticated in the region of the Mediterranean and giving the landscape its characteristic stamp. *A. victoriae reginae* is the showpiece of every small or large collection. It can be grown in the greenhouse, indoors as well as outdoors in the garden in the summer months. It should be planted in heavier, nourishing soil and supplied with sufficient light and water during the growth period. In winter it should be kept in a light, dry environment at a temperature of 5—7°C (41—45°F). Propagation is from the seed.

94

Aloe concinna BAK.

Aloes are a group of succulent species very like the American agaves. They are widespread throughout all of Africa, the Mediterranean region, Arabia, Madagascar and Zanzibar. Their numbers increase and the succulence is greater in the southern areas of the range. Aloes are marked by a great diversity of shape, some having the leaves arranged in two rows or forming rosettes close to the ground, some in the form of shrubs and others having stems up to 30 feet (10 metres) high branching broadly at the top. The leaves contain a yellowish or brown juice which thickens into a brown resin known to the Greeks as a potent drug as early as the 4th century B.C. Best suited for the preparation of the drug were the species *A. africana*, *A. ferox*, *A. plicatilis* and *A. vera*. In the Orient aloes were used for embalming.

Best suited for cultivation are the short or ornamental species. Little known is *Aloe concinna* of Zanzibar. The narrow lanceolate leaves arranged in a rosette are up to 6 inches (15 centimetres) long, 1 inch (2.5 centimetres) wide, and pale green in colour. Their outer surface is convex, and covered with white elongate spots. The edges are toothed and the tip curves downwards slightly. The leaves dry from the base upwards and fall off in age, leaving a short, fairly small stem. The flowers are in the form of a simple or compound raceme, up to 10 inches (25 centimetres) long, on short stalks. They are tube-shaped and coloured yellow-pink with a green edge.

A. concinna is a hardy, undemanding plant with a slow growth. It likes a warm and light situation; in summer it requires sufficient water but does not tolerate direct sunlight; on the other hand it is not affected by the dusty, smoke-filled atmosphere of the city. In winter it should be kept in a light place at a temperature of about 10°C (50°F) and water should be applied sparingly, just enough to prevent the plant from becoming too dry. It can be propagated successfully from the shoots growing from the base.

The specific name *concinna* means gentle, lovely.

Aloe variegata L.

Aloe variegata forms thick rosettes up to 12 inches (30 centimetres) high with slantingly ascending leaves spirally arranged in three rows. The leaves are triangular, indented on the inner side, and coloured grey-green with whitish spots. They measure 5 inches (12 centimetres) or more in length and up to $1\frac{1}{2}$ inches (3.5 centimetres) in width. The edges are bordered with fine white gristly teeth. The flower raceme comprises twenty to thirty meaty-red to scarlet-purple, green-edged flowers. Larger plants flower every year in spring and early summer three to six times.

A. *variegata*, commonly known as the "Falcon Feather" or "Tiger Aloe", is perhaps the loveliest of all and has been cultivated for many decades in window gardens growing in the company of nutmeg and clivia. Today this colourful, white-spotted succulent is a popular ornamental and is propagated on a large scale in horticultural establishments. Here it is grown from the seed which has good powers of germination and attains full growth within two to three years. It can also be propagated with ease from the underground shoots, found in ample numbers on older and larger plants. It requires a heavier, nourishing soil and a situation with ample light. It does not tolerate direct sunlight, continual damp and cold, especially in winter when it is liable to lose its roots.

A. *variegata* comes from Cape Province, the home of many interesting and ornamental species. The specific name *variegata* means variegated.

98

Caralluma europaea N. E. BR.

The genus *Caralluma* comprises more than 130 species and varieties with a large range of distribution embracing South and North Africa, Ethiopia, Somalia, Sudan, Arabia, the Island of Sokotra in the Indian Ocean and east India. The plants are small shrubs often bearing flowers that are beautifully coloured but have an odious scent. They are usually cultivated only by specialists.

Caralluma europaea makes low shrubs with branches 4 inches (10 centimetres) high and up to $\frac{3}{4}$ inch (1.5 centimetres) thick. These are quadrilateral, bluntly toothed and green in colour, strewn with greenish-brown flecks. The flowers emerge during the summer usually at the tip of the shoot in clusters of ten or more. The individual flowers are small, five pointed, $\frac{1}{2}-\frac{3}{4}$ inch (1—1.5 centimetres) across, pale brown with brownish-red stripes.

C. europaea is cultivated like the *Stapelia*. It does well in dry, modern homes in company with other ornamentals or in glass window cases with other succulents. During the growing period it requires sufficient light, moisture and warmth; in winter a light, dry atmosphere and a temperature of 5—8°C (41—46°F). It can be propagated successfully from the shoots removed in May or June. The cut surfaces must be left to dry in the sun for about fourteen days after which they are put in pots filled with sandy soil where they soon take root. It is also easily grown from the seed which germinates within a few days in a warm and moist environment.

The native habitat is the Island of Lampedusa in the Mediterranean, but its range includes both the east and west coasts of Africa as well as the southern coast of Spain, home of *C. europaea* var. *confusa*. This is the northernmost point of the species' distribution.

Ceropegia sandersonii DECNE

Succulents comprise plants of such a variety of shapes that even the smallest collection is certain to be admired by the layman. Members of the genus *Ceropegia* are no exception to the rule, even though they cannot rival the diversity of *Euphorbia* or *Kalanchoe*. They are popular plants cultivated mainly for the interesting lantern-like flowers. In the main they make semi-shrubs with fleshy, pendent or creeping branches. The flowers are funnel-shaped, swollen at the base, pentagonal at the top, and of different colours. A fairly widespread species is *Ceropegia sandersonii* of Natal, South Africa. It has strong creeping branches about ¼ inch (5 millimetres) thick, often as much as 6 feet (2 metres) long and coloured green. The leaves are thick, 1—2 inches (3—5 centimetres) long, green, heart-shaped, opposite (paired) on short stalks, spaced 4—8 inches (10—20 centimetres) apart. The flowers, also borne on short stalks, are pale green, up to 3 inches (7 centimetres) long and up to 1¾ inches (4.5 centimetres) across, swollen at the base and pentagonal at the top. When open the flower resembles a parachute coloured green with darker spots on the outside. The edges are toothed and bordered with white moving hairs. The flowers emerge in the top part of the plant throughout the summer until late autumn.

C. sandersonii requires a support for its creeping branches, good nourishing soil, warmth and light. During the growing period water should be supplied in sufficient doses. The plant is propagated well from the shoots which quickly take root.

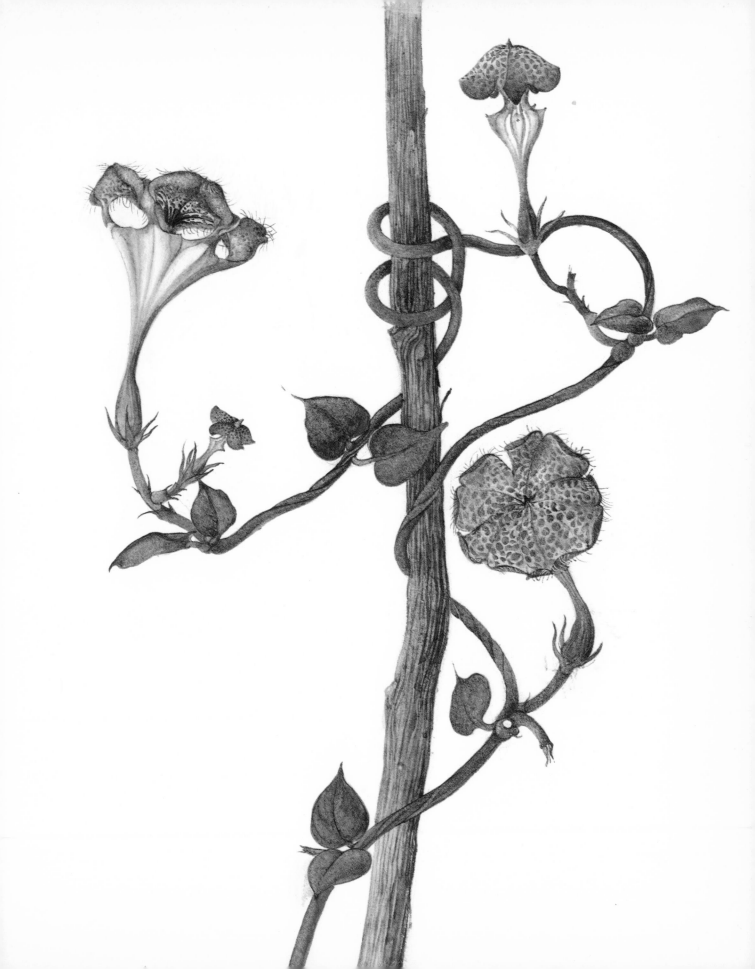

Cotyledon undulata HAW.

The genus *Cotyledon* has several interesting species, some of which are classed as rarities, grown only by specialists or in botanical gardens. They are true gems, most of them coming from Cape Province. One group comprises short, very succulent shrubs with thick, short branches and small deciduous leaves, for example *Cotyledon bucholziana*, *C. reticulata*, *C. pearsonii* and *C. ventricosa*. The last two are poisonous.

The second, more attractive group is distinguished by the white, chalky bloom on the leaves. Best known from this group are *C. orbiculata* with its attractive varieties *C. orbiculata* var. *ausana*, *C. orbiculata* var. *dinteri* and *C. orbiculata* var. *higginsiae*, and *C. undulata* with wavy-edged leaves.

This plant grows as bushes up to 20 inches (50 centimetres) high; in cultivation it grows singly, rarely making shoots from the base. The leaves are thick, fleshy, 3—5 inches (8—12 centimetres) long, $2\frac{1}{2}$ inches (6 centimetres) wide, oval, the edges wavy towards the tip with heavy chalky bloom. The flower stalk is 12—16 inches (30—40 centimetres) high, the flowers small, 1 inch (2.5 centimetres) long, and golden-orange.

C. undulata occurs also in the variety var. *mucronata* which has smaller leaves with a reddish-brown margin.

Well-cultivated plants are truly beautiful and very delicate. When transplanting or transferring the plants from one spot to another great care must be taken not to rub off the chalky bloom. Water, too, must not come in contact with the leaves and therefore should be applied only to the soil, care being taken never to sprinkle the plant. *C. undulata* should be grown in a sunny position in heavier, clay soil. It tolerates high temperatures and in winter requires a dry, light atmosphere with a temperature of about 10°C (50°F). It is propagated well from cuttings or from the leaves; in large-scale propagation, from the seed.

Crassula arborescens (MILL.) WILLD.

The genus *Crassula* comprises more than three hundred species including some of the best-known succulents, and rare ones such as *Crassula alstonii, C. arta, C. columella, C. columnaris, C. hemisphaerica, C. mesembryanthemopsis, C. pyramidalis, C. teres* and others which are cultivated only by specialists. The majority come from Cape Province or South-west Africa.

For better orientation A. Berger divided the genus *Crassula* into seven sections and these, in turn, into groups according to their relationship. These include clump-like species, low shrub-like species, shrubs or "trees" with thick, fleshy branches attaining a height of 13 feet (4 metres).

The largest species of all is *Crassula arborescens* of Cape Province. Berger assigned it to the Stellatae, group Arborea, which also includes *C. obliqua* and *C. portulacea*, attaining a height of 10 feet (3 metres). *C. arborescens* is a robust shrub or "tree" up to 13 feet (4 metres) high. The thick fleshy branches bear fleshy, blunt-tipped, ovoid leaves, 1½ inches (3.5 centimetres) across and 3 inches (7 centimetres) long, coloured pale grey-green, the upper surface spotted with small red-brown dots and the margins bordered with red. The flowers appearing in June to July are white at first, later tinged with pink. *C. arborescens* is cultivated as an ornamental household plant from 10—12 inches (25—30 centimetres) high. It is well suited for dry, light modern homes. Propagation is usually by cuttings with three to four pairs of leaves planted immediately in sandy, porous soil.

The specific name *arborescens* means tree-like.

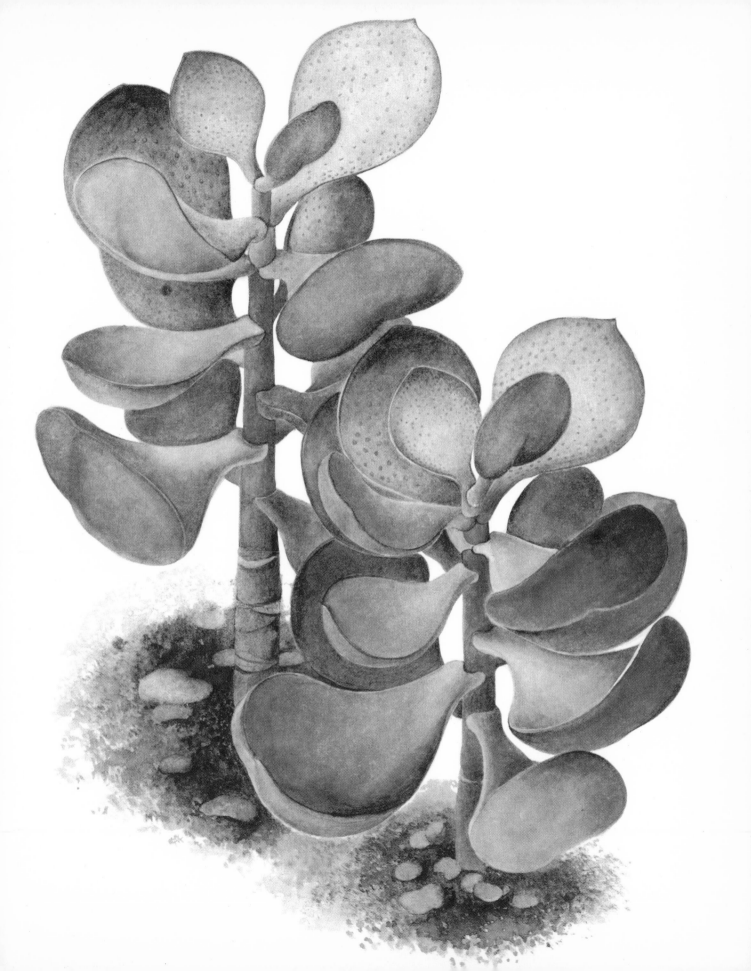

Crassula perforata THUNBG.

Belonging to an entirely different group of crassulas are the pendent, shrub-like species assigned by A. Berger to the Campanulatae, group Perforata. Other well-known species included in this group are *Crassula brevifolia* — a small, delicate, shrub-like plant with thick boat-shaped leaves edged with red; *C. marnieriana* — with branches covered with small, closely set leaves; and *C. conjuncta* — very like, but smaller than *C. perforata*.

C. perforata, also known as *perfossa*, makes small shrubs of prostrate, fleshy, later woody stems. The pairs of leaves are joined, broadly ovate, with short pointed tip, at right angles to the stem, $\frac{1}{2}$—$\frac{3}{4}$ inch (1.5—2 centimetres) long, and $\frac{1}{3}$—$\frac{1}{2}$ inch (9—13 millimetres) wide. The colour is pale grey-green, with a red border and numerous small reddish dots in the sun. The small, whitish flowers emerge in spring. The plant's native habitat is Cape Province.

C. perforata is a popular succulent grown also as a hanging plant. The smaller *C. conjuncta* with pendent stems is likewise grown in this manner. In the past years a large number of less spreading hybrid species of *C. perforata* have been gaining in popularity. These all do well in light, warm rooms, although direct sunlight weakens them. In winter they require a light, dry environment and temperature of 7—10°C (45—50°F). *C. perforata* is propagated with ease from the shoots which should be planted into rich, porous soil where they take root within two to three weeks.

Euphorbia grandicornis GOEBEL.

Euphorbia grandicornis of Africa is a striking succulent easily grown in cultivation. It makes thick branched bushes comprising triangular, winged, pale green branches slanting upwards from the stem. The edges are wavy with light brown border which later turns dark brown. The thick, horn-shaped spines, arranged in pairs, are up to 2 inches (5 centimetres) long, pale brown, later grey. The flowers are small and yellow, the fruit red.

This plant grows in several parts of Africa — Natal, Tanzania, Kenya. In Europe, especially in greenhouses, it grows to an imposing height of 3—6 feet (1—2 metres). Even though it attains large dimensions, under good conditions it is well suited for cultivation in dry, warm and light homes as long as there is adequate space.

The specific name *grandicornis* means large-horned, after the large, thick spines.

Euphorbias have one trait in common — when wounded all exude a white, poisonous milk that must not come in contact with the eye or an open wound. This characteristic is the reason why euphorbias are attacked by very few pests in the wild and why they remain healthy and undamaged, unmolested by game even in regions where there is a lack of pasture land and water.

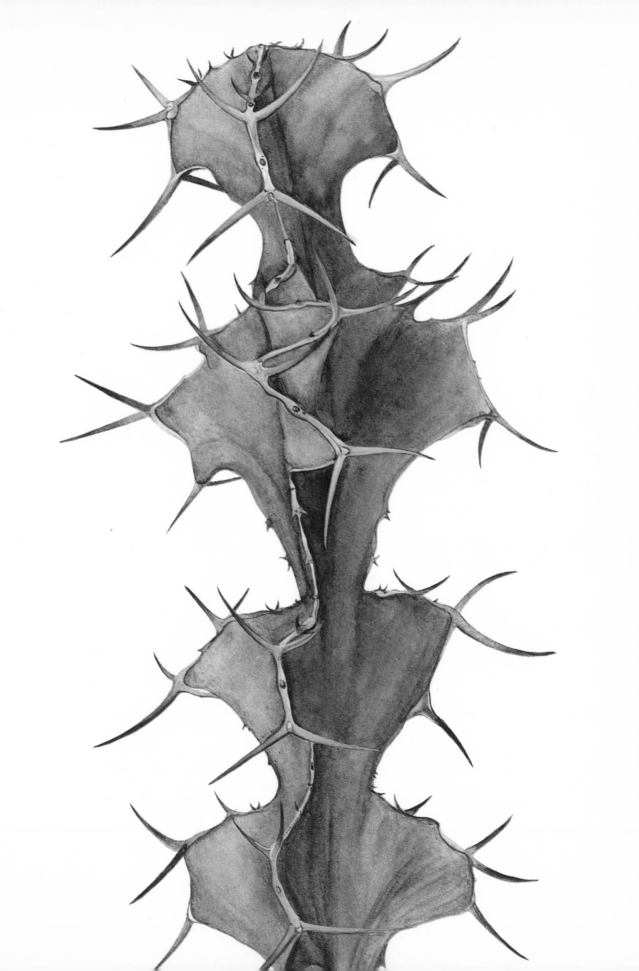

Euphorbia horrida BOISS.

This interesting species from South Africa shows a marked resemblance to the spiny cactus. Spherical in youth, about 6 inches (15 centimetres) across, it becomes columnar in age, attaining a height of 3 feet (1 metre). The skin is dark green tinged with grey. Older plants are corky at the base. The ribs, about twelve, are narrow with toothed edges and covered with groups of spines, $\frac{1}{2}$—$\frac{3}{4}$ inch (1—2 centimetres) long, set $\frac{1}{2}$—$\frac{3}{4}$ inch apart. *E. horrida* is a dioecious plant with small, nondescript flowers. The specific name *horrida*, meaning frightening, was apparently prompted by the thorny flower stalks.

It is highly prized by growers specializing in succulents, as are *E. obesa*, *E. buplerifolia* and *E. fasciculata*. In its native land it is used as a host plant for the parasitic mistletoe *Viscum minimum* which has beautiful bright red flowers and fruit. The seeds of *Viscum* are pressed into the grooves between the ribs where they soon germinate and the roots penetrate into the plant tissue. Small shoots and leaves appear in the second year.

E. horrida is not difficult to grow and if at least the minimum requirements are respected it does well in light, dry households with adequate sunlight. The temperature should be about 10—15°C (50—60°F) even in winter. Propagation is easy from the shoots or from the seed.

Euphorbia obesa HOOK. F.

The first specimens of *Euphorbia obesa* were sent to England in 1897 to the botanical gardens at Kew under the name *Euphorbia meloformis*. Despite the many characteristics it had in common with *E. meloformis*, Professor Hooker soon discovered a number of differences and in 1903 described it as the new species *Euphorbia obesa*.

E. obesa is a spherical, pale green plant, brownish-green with reddish-brown stripes in the sun; in age it has a columnar growth attaining a height of 6 inches (15 centimetres). Like many succulent euphorbias it bears either all pistillate or all staminate blooms, thus making it necessary to have both types for seed.

Imports to Europe in the first years all died for want of knowledge of the conditions in which they grew in their native habitat. It was not until young plants better adapted to the new environment were cultivated from the seed that the species ceased being such a great rarity. Even though *E. obesa* is more widespread today it still remains a rarity in cultivation because of the difficulty of acquiring the seed. As a rule every pistillate flower has one three-part ovary which bursts when ripe ejecting the seed to a distance of as much as 3 feet (1 metre). For good growth *E. obesa* requires a sunny, warm site. It should be planted in porous, clay soil with a larger portion of crushed brick. In winter it should be placed in a light, dry spot with a temperature of 12—15°C (54—59°F). Propagation is only from the seed; germinating seedlings are sensitive to damp.

Fenestraria rhopalophylla N. E. BR.

The genus *Fenestraria* (window plants) established by N. E. Brown is very aptly named. The "window" leaves serve to disperse the sun's rays on to the tissues containing chlorophyll, located inside the leaf. This genus is very interesting both from the biological and morphological aspects. In its native habitat in Cape Province the greater part of the plant is underground with only the leaf tips with their translucent panes above the surface. It is thus that the plant protects itself against the scorching sun and pests.

Fenestraria rhopalophylla makes a rosette of long, cylindrical leaves, and later forms clumps about 4 inches (10 centimetres) across and 2 inches (5 centimetres) high. The leaves are pale green, club-shaped at the tip, $\frac{1}{4}$—$\frac{1}{2}$ inch (0.5—1 centimetre) thick, terminating in a convex, almost circular, mat green "window". The pure white flowers measure 2 inches (5 centimetres) across and are borne on stalks 2 inches (5 centimetres) in length.

Very similar in appearance with only slight differences is the species *Fenestraria aurantiaca* which bears yellow-orange flowers about $2\frac{3}{4}$ inches (7 centimetres) across.

Both species flower in autumn, from August to October. During the growing period they require ample sun, heat and careful watering. In winter a dry atmosphere, light and a temperature of 10—15°C (50—59°F) are necessary. They are propagated well from the seed.

Frithia pulchra N. E. BR.

Frithia pulchra is likewise a "window" plant. It forms small rosettes of ten or more, dark green leaves, about $1\frac{1}{2}$ inches (3.5 centimetres) long, cylindrical, with a shallow groove down the entire length, terminating in a light, mat "window". The flowers emerge in the centre of the plant, are carmine-red with a white centre and measure about $\frac{3}{4}$ inch (2 centimetres) across. The specific name *pulchra* means beautiful.

The genus *Frithia* has only one species which is fairly hardy. During the growth period that is from spring till summer, it requires a warm sunny site and careful watering, and during the rest period light and a dry atmosphere. The ground should be slightly dampened, to prevent the plant from becoming too dry. It should be planted in small flower pots in porous soil with the leaves above the surface. The pots are placed in crushed brick or sand. Propagation is from the seed which has good powers of germination. The seedlings mature in two to three years.

Gasteria armstrongii SCHOENL.

Gasteria of the family Liliaceae are popular succulents. The plants grow in clumps. The leaves are thick, rigid, tongue-shaped or elongate, dark green with white spots or warts. The various species are distinguished by the shape and size of the leaves and flowers. The native habitat is Cape Province and South-west Africa where more than eighty species are known to grow.

One of the best known is *Gasteria armstrongii*, named after the botanist W. Armstrong. The thick, leathery, dark green, warty leaves are tongue-shaped and are arranged in two rows. New leaves are erect at first, later appressed to the older leaves which grow horizontally. Rarely do they grow to more than 4 inches (10 centimetres) in length. Older plants make side shoots. The flowers are small pink tubes arranged in a raceme about 12 inches (30 centimetres) long.

The first twelve specimens were grown at the botanical garden in Vienna in 1912 from the twelve seeds sent there by W. Armstrong that same year. From there the plant spread to other botanical gardens and private collections throughout Europe. Because of its ease of cultivation, hardiness and small dimensions, *G. armstrongii* is well suited for cultivation in the household, in both small and large collections. Like all the *Gasteria* it does not tolerate a scorching sun and continually dry atmosphere. It is propagated well from the young shoots which grow on the sides of older plants, but these are few in number. The plant should be isolated from other species of *Gasteria* to prevent unwanted hybridization. The seeds have good powers of germination and the plants mature within two to three years. They should be grown in heavier, porous, clay soil.

Gasteria maculata (THUNBG.) HAW.

The eighty species of *Gasteria* include a number of interesting and attractive plants that deserve greater attention on the part of growers and which would make a nice collection in themselves. One of the most decorative is *Gasteria maculata* from Cape Province, South Africa.

The specific name *maculata* indicates that the plant has spotted leaves. These are arranged in two rows, often spirally. They are stiff, thick, about 8 inches (20 centimetres) long, with a flat or convex surface strewn with white spots that are pinkish in the sun. The flowers are arranged in a loose raceme about 12 inches (30 centimetres) long. The individual flowers are tubular, swollen at the base, red with a green border. They appear several times during the year and last fairly long.

G. maculata is a popular succulent well suited to dry, modern homes. It thrives in any spot without direct sunlight, even in spots where other plants will not grow, like facing north-west or north-east. The first flowers appear in early spring, frequently as early as the end of February and March. In summer there is a brief dormant period when the plants should be given only enough water to keep them from becoming too dry. Watering is resumed from September till the end of October. In winter they should be kept in a dry cool spot at a temperature of 5—10°C (41—50°F). Some nurseries cultivate *Gasteria* on a large scale but only a limited assortment, although they are easy to propagate from the shoots or leaf cuttings. Propagation from the seed is not recommended because of the ease of hybridization with other species and the possibility that it would not come true. *Gasteria* do well in heavier, rich, porous, clay soil.

Haworthia fasciata (WILLD.) HAW.

Haworthia fasciata or one of its varieties or forms is one of the basic plants of every collection of succulents.

It forms rosettes of leaves about 3 inches (8 centimetres) across making side shoots at the base. The leaves are glossy, green, 1½—2½ inches (4—6 centimetres) long, about ½ inch (13 millimetres) wide, triangular, elongate, and flat on the upper side. The underside is convex with large white warts arranged in horizontal rows. The small whitish flowers are arranged in an upright raceme about 12—16 inches (30—40 centimetres) high. They emerge several times in the year. The habitat is South Africa.

This large genus was named in honour of the British scientist and collector of succulents Adrian Hardy Haworth. It was always an object of study on the part of experts and scientists, especially in England, Germany, Holland, the USA and South Africa. H. Jacobsen places *H. fasciata* in the section Margaretifera which includes the most attractive species of the whole genus, *H. attenuata*, with its many varieties, the prettiest being var. *clariperla* with large white warts arranged in loose horizontal bands. A great favourite is *H. margaretifera* which has a large number of varieties differing from each other only slightly. It is somewhat more spreading, with broader leaves covered with large white warts arranged in loose horizontal bands.

H. fasciata and other striped haworthias are popular and widely cultivated not only by growers of cacti and other succulents but mainly by youngsters because of their ease of cultivation. It does well almost everywhere, although it does not tolerate direct sunlight or a dry atmosphere during the growth period for this causes the leaf tips to dry. The growth period is from March until May, followed by the summer rest period until the end of August, during which time water should only be applied sparingly, just enough to prevent the plant from becoming too dry. September marks the beginning of a new growth period. In winter water should be applied lightly and only occasionally until spring, and the temperature should be kept at 6—10°C (43—50°F).

H. fasciata is propagated with ease from the rosettes which arise at the base of older plants. It is grown from the seed only when purity of the species is assured, for it hybridizes easily.

Haworthia truncata SCHOENL.

The desert regions of South Africa where the temperature of the ground is between 50—60°C (122—140°F) at noon and where there is a great dearth of water are the home of a large number of odd succulents which have adapted themselves to the harsh environment. Besides a high degree of succulence they have a special device which serves to protect them from the intense solar radiation. This device, a sort of "window", is also to be found in *H. truncata*.

Haworthia truncata is a small, short succulent plant rarely larger than 2½ inches (6 centimetres). It consists of two rows of thick, dark green leaves. The small whitish flowers arise in the centre of the plant and are arranged in a loose raceme 8—12 inches (20—30 centimetres) long.

H. truncata is without doubt one of the most interesting of the succulents. The thick leaves have a sort of transparent "window" on the truncated tip of each leaf which lets in only a certain amount of the sun's rays necessary for assimilation. In its habitat, that is, in Cape Province, South Africa, the plant is buried in the ground up to the transparent leaf tips, thus protecting itself against the intense solar radiation. Its remarkable shape and small size make it a great favourite with growers, although it is a species which requires particular care and therefore its cultivation is recommended only to experienced growers. Dr. K. von Poellnitz differentiated the rare and little-known forms *crassa*, *normalis* and *tenuis* according to the varying shape and size of the "window".

H. truncata should be planted in heavier, porous soil up to the leaves. Water should be applied sparingly especially during the summer rest period when the soil should be only slightly moist. In winter it requires light, a dry atmosphere and a temperature of about 10°C (50°F). Propagation is usually from the seed.

The specific name *truncata* means truncated.

Lithops aucampiae L. BOL.

These are very succulent plants growing in arid desert regions, their whole bodies except for the crown concealed in sand or gravel which protects them from the heat of the sun. The body shape and coloration serve to reflect and disperse most of the sun's rays, permitting only the necessary amount to penetrate and be transmitted by a clear fluid to the layer of chlorophyll grains located inside the body along the edge of the plant. The process of assimilation in this instance takes place underground, a unique phenomenon in the plant realm.

Lithops aucampiae is an inconspicuous, reddish-brown plant pressed close to the ground, its stems resembling pebbles so that it is difficult to find in the wild. The stems are about ¾ inch (2 centimetres) high and 1 inch (3 centimetres) wide, divided by a shallow slit into two unequal halves. Near the slit are dark green "windows". The flowers are yellow, about 1 inch (2.5 centimetres) across. The habitat is the Transvaal.

Lithops mickbergensis DTR.

Lithops mickbergensis has two joined leaves forming a conical stem about 1½ inches (4 centimetres) high and narrowing towards the root. The leaf tips are truncated and circular, about 1 inch (2.5 centimetres) in diameter. The flowers are white and arise from the centre of the slit. This plant comes from South-west Africa.

"Live Stones", as they are popularly called, require sunlight throughout the whole day and will even tolerate a temperature of 50°C (122°F) without damage. The soil should be porous with good drainage to provide for rapid dispersion of excess water. The plants should be placed in small flower pots which are put in sand with peat, brick rubble, etc., so that the delicate roots do not become too dry. During the growth period, that is from April until September, water should be applied sparingly, only enough to keep the soil slightly moist. In winter *Lithops* require a dry atmosphere and adequate light; the temperature, however, may be as low as 8—10°C (46—50°F). The flowers appear in autumn and open in sunlight in the afternoon. Propagation is only from the seed; seedlings mature within two to three years.

Stapelia grandiflora MASS.

Stapelia grandiflora is another succulent from Cape Province. It is a typical species distinguished by its interesting shape and the size of the flowers which gave it its name. It is cultivated by specialists together with other species of *Stapelia*, *Caralluma*, *Trichocaulon*, *Hoodia*, and the like. These succulents are widely cultivated especially in England, Holland and Germany.

This plant forms clumps of quadrangular stems up to 12 inches (30 centimetres) high, $1—1\frac{1}{2}$ inches (3—4 centimetres) thick, intense green, and covered with fine hairs. The edges of the stems are compressed and toothed, with small pointed leaves. Several pointed, swollen, pink buds on short stalks arise in a group at the base of each new shoot. The flowers are about 6 inches (15 centimetres) across, the corolla lobes are triangular, wrinkled, pale purple, horizontally striped, and thickly covered with soft grey hairs.

S. grandiflora is easy to cultivate. It grows just as well in the sun as in partial shade, bearing a profusion of flowers every year, several to a shoot. The large purple flowers have an unpleasant smell reminiscent of decaying meat which attracts flies that pollinate the blooms and lay eggs at the same time. *S. grandiflora* should be grown in heavier, porous, clay soil. Propagation is from the shoots which are left to dry for several days in the sun and then planted in sandy, clay soil. The plants can also be grown from the seed which has good and rapid powers of germination. The seedlings have delicate roots at the beginning and bear flowers within three years.

Stapelia variegata L.

Stapelia variegata, likewise from South Africa, differs markedly from *Stapelia grandiflora* both in the shape of the shoots as well as in the size, shape and colour of the flowers. It forms thick clumps of short stems, about 4 inches (10 centimetres) long, coloured green to grey-green, often reddish, with narrow erect teeth. One to five pale green, swollen buds borne on short stalks about 2 inches (5 centimetres) long, emerge at the base of each new shoot. The flower is flat, fleshy, 2—3 inches (5—8 centimetres) across, wrinkled, dull yellow inside with dark brown spots scattered over the surface or arranged in irregular rows. Inside the flower is a thick, somewhat rounded ring, coloured dull yellow with small brown spots. The corolla lobes are broadly ovate, sharp-tipped, bending back in time.

Specialized collections contain about twenty-five varieties showing only slight differences in the patterning of the flowers. The ease of hybridization raises doubts about many of these varieties. After fertilization, usually through the medium of flies attracted by the smell like decaying meat exuded by the flowers, each blossom turns into two shells containing flat, pale brown seeds covered with silvery, silky, glossy hairs. The seeds are carried by the wind to great distances.

Only a few succulents adapt so easily to different conditions in cultivation as does *S. variegata*, for which reason it is very popular, especially with beginners. It is propagated with ease from shoots which quickly take root and bear a wealth of stiff, leathery flowers resembling stars throughout the whole summer until late autumn. It will thrive in any situation, in the sun or in partial shade. In winter it requires a dry atmosphere and light; the temperature may drop to 2—3°C (36—37°F).